SAILING ON A RAINBOW

A colourful journey with Autism

BY ADESOLA TOYIN ADESOKAN

CONTENTS

ক্রপ্ত

YES, HE WILL

I have a child said to have special needs
The state struggles with aiming high. the
community questions your parenting style
For your child to have tuned out this way,
you do not know, do you?

You do not know what it means to fight
fear and embrace faith. You do not know
what it means to stay strong when your
body is crying "give up!"

You do not know what it means to have
to stay firm with your child when your
heart yells to be tender with him

You do not know what it means to
be determined to have lofty expectations in
situations when statistics seem to say aim low

You do not know what it means to
become an expert because you have
researched so much into possibilities

SAILING ON A RAINBOW

That it is possible

For a child who seems so far behind to
become the top of the class

For a child who has been written off to
become the one is winning all

For a child who did not talk to become
the one who tells it all

Oh! The battle seems so hard with
hopelessness and criticisms staring at me
But I refuse to give in, I refuse to give up

I choose to rise like an edifice higher and
higher so that this child of mine can stand
on my shoulder to see that indeed the
the world is for the taking and to go on to
take the world despite the said
limitations.

INTRODUCTION

Where do I begin telling the tale of Ade's journey with autism?

It is a journey of twist and turns, with moments of boundless joy and moments of total despair. It is a journey that nothing could have prepared me for, yet there is no room to sit around and complain, or to invite others to celebrate my self-pity. I must get up, take courage and forge ahead, trusting that the choices I make for Ade along this uncharted path will lead him to a worthy destination.

For a long time, I used to tease Ade that one day I would sit down and write books about the rollercoaster of emotions I experienced in raising him. These emotions were not really about things he did, or did not do, but were instead about what I felt he should have been but was not. He was just being himself, but I often found it difficult to accept him for who he was. An avalanche of information on the odds stacked up against Ade left me in deep trepidation about his future.

I wanted to document these emotions and experiences in a book, but the daily realities of running a home limited the time available to write. The motivation came as I listened one day to the plea of a mother, desperate to get support in raising a child recently diagnosed with autism. It made me think about the struggles and triumphs of countless parents and carers like me. I realised that my story could help other parents and carers. Some of these parents and carers I met when coming to terms with Ade's diagnosis with an autism spectrum disorder/condition (I say autism) and its ramifications, others I have read about or listened to, while others I may never meet.

One thing that became clear was that I could no longer wait for a perfect time to tell Ade's story. I had to help others navigating the often confusing world of parents and carers raising children diagnosed with autism. I just knew I had to put pen to paper.

It is, therefore, my desire that the words you read in the next few pages as I sketch out Ade's journey with autism will bring hope and courage to your heart and mind, whether you are raising a child diagnosed with autism or facing other challenges. I choose to believe that all things are possible.

THE PRINCE IS BORN

Almost thirteen years ago, I held in my hands a bundle of joy and the exhilaration was beyond expression. This was no ordinary child. This was Ade, whom I would raise to be a complete gentleman. He weighed 4.14 kg at birth, though he was quite slender, and his frame was exceptionally long. He was and still is a beauty to behold. Ilerioluwa (God's promise) Adegbemiro (Sustained by royalty), Ade (as he likes to be called), my handsome prince had come to complete our kingdom, for our princess (Ademurewa) had earlier taken her place. His arrival was a joyful fulfilment of our dream, and my husband was particularly thankful to have an "heir".

Ade was never one to be ignored. Even at the hospital where he was born, he refused to leave my side, and any attempt to put him in a cot was met with ceaseless cries. The nurses would try taking him away for a while with the hope that he would settle in his cot, but not Ade. As soon as he was placed in the cot the wailing began, but once by my side he was a contented and happy baby.

The nurses were left with no choice but to allow him to sleep by my side. They had to allow him, if only to give some respite to the other courageous women who were fighting to bring forth their babies, whether for the first or umpteenth time, and for the sake of the babies themselves, who were experiencing the world for the first time.

I thought the many cries I had heard Ade raise at the hospital were a sign of things to come when we were discharged from the hospital, but Ade proved me wrong. Instead, he turned out to be a peaceful baby, an easy to nurture baby. His feeding was very considerate, and his sleeping allowed me to get on with other things without much ado from him.

Going out with Ade was a pure pleasure. Everyone who saw him remarked on how handsome he was. Many even mistook him for a girl and declared, "Your daughter is so beautiful." When his dad and I would point out that he was a boy, they still insisted that "beautiful" was the most suitable word! That always painted rays of sunshine all over our faces and put indescribable joy in our hearts.

The first year of Ade's life was full of joy and laughter as he hit the expected milestones right on time. He smiled! He sat! He crawled! He walked! These were all moments full of smiles and happiness. To crown it all, he started chatting and responding to conversations! My joy knew no bounds as his voice reverberated around the house.

Although he was an active baby, there was something intriguing about him. Ade had moments when he appeared to be completely lost in deep reflection. It was as if he knew he was on a mission in this world and he was searching for ways to fulfil it. It was a real pleasure to behold. However, this joy was short-lived, as my excitement soon turned into a period of despair.

> LESSON LEARNT: For months before the Ade's birth, I worried that I might not be able to love him as deeply as I loved my daughter because I thought I had given all the love I had to share to my daughter. This worry came to nothing. From the moment I saw Ade, I became consumed with love so powerful that my heart yearned to hold him and never let him go. Then I realised that:

- Each born child is unique and wrapped with a blanket of love that melts your heart at first sight.

- Having a child is gloriously challenging. Yes, babies are a joy to hold and to have, but they also have the power to rock your world as they test the depth of your strength, tenacity and resourcefulness with their endless demands.

One then wonders, how is it that a job as diverse and challenging as raising children comes without training?

THE LIGHT WENT OUT

When Ade was about 18 months old, we started to be puzzled. I wondered what was happening. Can a child forget words he has been using? Wait a minute! Why is he no longer responding to his name, or to anything else? It was like the light had gone out of Ade's eyes and he had started to shut down. I turned to my husband for answers, but his guess was as good as mine.

No matter what we were doing at home, Ade stopped showing any interest. He used to play with his sister, but no longer wanted to. Before, when I sang to him, he would smile, and you could see the sparkle in his eyes. When I tickled him, he would giggle and laugh as if to say, "Don't stop Mum, I'm having so much fun!" But no more. No more smiles, no more laughter and no more sparkles. Instead, total silence, blankness and more silence. The silence became so loud that it was deafening.

So, with his dad's consent, I took Ade to the baby clinic, as I had before. But this time was different. This time I had an urgent story to tell. This time, I needed an audience and I had a riddle to be solved.

I collected my thoughts and explained to the health visitor the drama unfolding before my eyes. I explained how Ade's words seemed to be disappearing! I told her how the boy I was holding was becoming less and less responsive to everything, even to his name, and appeared to be escaping into his own world that I couldn't understand. The health visitor examined him and noted he appeared to be a contented child, but that, if my concerns persisted, she recommended I should contact my GP.

How could I make the health visitor, or anyone understand how it felt to watch the light go out of your son's eyes? How could I make them understand that the once bubbling child had become a shadow of himself? Yes, Ade was still here, but he was not here. He was healthy so I could understand why all the health visitor saw was a contented child, while his dad and I saw a child whose soul and mind we could no longer reach, preventing any form of deep emotional connection.

I took my precious son back home no less confused than before but more determined than ever to find an answer. I spent more time playing with him, I read more books to him, I spoke more with him, I sang him more songs, gave him more tickles and I played him his favourite nursery rhymes, and so did his dad. But there was no sound, no light and no acknowledgement, only a child who seemed lost.

It was a very lonely time for his dad and I because no one else seemed to know or feel what we were dealing with. No one knew how brightly the light in Ade's eye had shone and how all we now saw was darkness. Some close family and friends felt Ade was just a "late bloomer" and that he would flourish in his own good time. While that was comforting, we knew instinctively that something wasn't right.

My mind was clouded with troubling thoughts and, no matter how hard I tried, I couldn't solve the riddle. What more could I do?

> LESSONS LEARNT: Many of us go into parenting thinking that we know what the rest of our lives are going to look like. We have this beautiful picture of the baby that we are bringing into the world and how it will fit into our lives.
>
> We may even go as far as dreaming what our child will look like, what career they will have and what life adventures are likely to await them.
>
> We fill our minds with countless dreams and expectations that are joyful and peaceful until we are sometimes awoken by a rude shock that:
>
> - Often, when our child enters into our world, they bring with them their own unique personality, talents, strengths and weaknesses.

- Who our child is and what they may become can have little to do with our dreams and expectations, and more to do with who the child is.

- Our dreams and expectations have been about us all along and not necessarily about our child. This is often a hard pill to swallow.

Consequently, this may leave us a little lost, a little confused, and more than a little disillusioned.

This was how I was feeling as I watched Ade retreat into his own unknown world. Rising above that and pushing aside my fears, disappointments, expectations and lost dreams seemed impossible. But would I admit defeat and continue to watch Ade become a total stranger? No! My love for him had to swallow up my fears and frustrations.

VISITS TO THE SPECIALISTS

Having decided that our GP could shine some light on our situation, I booked an appointment. So off to the GP I went. The GP listened carefully and, as he listened, he took copious notes. He also asked me questions such as, "When did he start talking?" and "When did I first notice he was losing his words?"

"What's the matter? Why the need for all this information? Why is the GP writing so much?" I wondered. Hold on, I tried to tell myself, as my mind continued to race in a thousand different directions. I tried to keep my cool but was a nerve-wracking wait.

After what seemed like forever, the GP finally straightened up and said he was making referrals to several specialists. He assured me that they would contact me shortly. "Why all these referrals?" I thought. Little did I know that this encounter with the GP was going to mark a turning point in our lives.

It began what I can only describe as a rollercoaster of emotions. It was thrilling, exhilarating, scary and mind-blowing.

It marked the beginning of a time when his dad and I found ourselves taking Ade from one specialist to another on this voyage of discovery. We thought one, or maybe two, visits to a specialist would solve the issue and lay the matter to rest. Little did we know that thoughts of a quick-fix to such a deep-rooted challenge might as well have qualified us as citizens of La-la-land.

But how could we have known? And what could have prepared us? We could never have imagined that regular visits to medical specialists was about to become our new normality.

The hearing specialist spent several minutes observing Ade under various conditions, using several kinds of equipment (including a cute toy soldier beating a tiny drum). Ade's hearing, noted the specialist, was functioning well so he had to discharge us. This apparently good news was devoid of comfort. Ade still uttered no word, nor responded. It was as if he was enveloped in a cloak of numb stillness.

I couldn't help but pin my hopes on the speech and language therapist to make the desired difference. So off we went as soon as we were given an appointment. Ade was fascinated by the sweet calming effect of the therapist's room. While the speech therapist was busy carrying out a comprehensive assessment of his speech, language and communication abilities, including social communication skills, Ade moved around the room softly picking up toys as if they were fragile and lining them up in a straight line.

The speech therapist wanted to see whether Ade had language and communication difficulties and whether she needed to conduct further assessment or to refer us to other services. She also said that she was part of the team that diagnosed autism and she needed to look at the presence or absence of autism. "What is she going on about?" I wondered. At the time, what she said made little sense to me.

The speech and language therapist continued to work with Ade to help him develop his communication and play skills. Ade didn't mind these sessions as he was oblivious to the true reason he was there. While Ade moved around the room, stopping from time to time, the therapist talked to him, read to him and played with him.

We were then referred to Portage. Portage is a home-visiting educational service for pre-school children with special education needs and disabilities (although I did not understand all this at the time). Our house became a play centre as the lovely Home Visitors from Portage came in to teach him how to play, while we still continued to attend our scheduled appointments with various medical specialists.

When all the specialists had conducted their assessments and made their findings, we also continued to meet with the paediatrician. I will never forget the many trips we made to the paediatrician as he assessed Ade, and as he worked to bring together all the reports of the various specialists.

The ultimate duty of the paediatrician, or so it seemed to us, was to find a solution to what was the matter with Ade. By now, Ade had completely shut down, and his soul seemed to have escaped to a world unknown, leaving him entirely unaware of his environment and of us!

LESSONS LEARNT: Some things in life have no quick fix. When we started visiting the specialists, I subconsciously felt they would instantly provide me with an understanding of why Ade had become the way he was and, more importantly, how it would magically go away. But I was wrong. We had to go from specialist to specialist in unravelling what was happening to Ade. Giving up, however, was not a possibility.

Looking back, it made a lot of difference that we recognised early that something was not quite right with Ade developmentally and made a swift decision to take him to the GP, who then made the relevant referrals to different specialists. This was crucial in ensuring he had early access to evidence-based interventions, such as speech and language therapy, play therapy and other types of interventions that are crucial to achieving more favourable life outcomes.

If a child is growing atypically, whether it is a delay in reaching expected milestones, having communication issues, unusual reactions to everyday things, or not responding to their name, as Ade had done, it is better to seek medical advice as early as possible to confirm what is or may be wrong or to reaffirm that there are no issues.

Being overly concerned about other people's impressions about you and your child must not be a reason to bury your head in the sand. Do not overlook it or keep silent about the problem for fear of stigmatisation or choose to "wait and watch". This will only postpone the help your child requires and increase your parental distress, which can have serious implications down the line.

We were told not to worry by people who were dear to us and who had the best of intentions, but we still acted on our instincts and took Ade to see the GP, and it was only there that we started to unravel the mystery. While admitting that something may be wrong with your child is not the easiest pill to swallow, you do need to be proactive, as early detection, I found, is key in helping a child with autism live a more normal and fulfilling life in society.

IT IS AUTISM!

Emotions flooded my mind and my world turned over as the paediatrician delivered the diagnosis. When Ade was three years old, the verdict was given. The paediatrician declared, "Autism it is!" The word was like a poisoned dagger piercing through my heart, almost shattering my soul.

"Never mind, you are the best people to take care of this child, as you have what it takes," declared the paediatrician to his dad and me in discharging us. It was like watching my entire world break into pieces. All I could do was sit still. I left the paediatrician's numbed as if anesthetised. I just could not feel anything. Numb to both pain and pleasure. Anyone who has been on the dentist's chair will understand what I am talking about. His dad sat motionless in total disbelief.

A kind couple from Burgess Autistic Trust (now known as Choice Support Autism) were with us at the paediatrician's office and were there when the diagnosis was delivered. (Choice Support Autism is a charity set up by a couple aimed at raising awareness about and providing advice and support to families with autistic children living in Bromley and South East London.) The couple tried to offer us some solace, as they had raised a child with autism and knew what it meant to hear that diagnosis. But I was so beside myself and so lost in my thoughts that I barely heard anything they said, though I was very grateful to have them. I am still grateful that they were there and also grateful to have them as our first friends in the new world of autism, sharing grief, laughter as well as crucial information. Gaining this information was later to become my lifelong quest.

LESSON LEARNT: Many parents experience scattered emotions preceding a grieving process on receiving the diagnosis of autism for their child. According to the well-known psychiatrist, Dr Elisabeth Kübler-Ross, "grief" she opined, occurs in five stages: Denial & Isolation, Anger, Depression, Bargaining, and Acceptance (Kubler-Ross, E. 1997). How insightful!

I, however, believe that what parents experience when they have a child diagnosed with autism is "cyclical grieving". This kind of grieving is said to be "cyclical" because of the reoccurring aspect of one or more emotions that are part of the first grieving process (Blaska, Joan.K. 1998) . These emotions may include anger, anxiety, denial, depression, disbelief, frustration, guilt, self-blame, helplessness, loneliness, nothingness, sadness and shock. These emotions come and go.

I believe having Ade diagnosed with autism was emotionally wrenching because we were confronting for the first time a condition, we knew very little about. At the same time, we were discharged from the services of the paediatrician who had just pronounced the verdict! The diagnosis felt like a jail sentence.

How could the pronouncement by the paediatrician that Ade had autism explain Ade's strengths, his concerns, his talents, his likes, his dislikes or the unique challenges and needs he might face? It did not. It just told me that Ade has been adjudged to fall within a range of a very broad spectrum of autism.

As much as I wanted to understand why Ade had become the way he was and help him access what he needed for his development, saying simply that he has autism can sometimes prevent him from getting the individualised services he needs. As Stephen Shore wisely said, *"If you've met one individual with autism, you've met one individual with autism."* For me as a parent, the failure of the diagnosis to present a holistic view of Ade was bewildering, like sending me further into the jungle with no compass.

Many parents in situations similar to or same as mine are given no guidance on what to do next. We were merely signposted to other services and moving on from the diagnosis was very daunting. We were thrown into the sea with no swimming lessons and no lifeboats. We had to learn to build the ship as we sailed. This, in turn, produced feelings of grief, stress and confusion.

Immediately, with no warning or preparation, our lives were transformed, and we had to learn a new way of living, as we needed to make more time for Ade, including the time needed for attending different therapies.

As this was stressful time for the whole family, there was a temptation to blame oneself, or one's partner, for the child having autism. Research has long discredited the "refrigerator mother" theory, a term coined by Leo Kanner and popularised by Bruno Bettelheim, which blamed parents, and especially the mother, by alleging that autism was caused by cold, uncaring parenting(Higham, P. 2020)).

We now know that autism has nothing to do with the parents' lifestyle, whether or not the child was planned, the parenting style adopted or how a parent displays affection towards the child.

The emotions experienced by parents when a child is diagnosed with autism are the symptoms of loss. It is the perceived loss of dreams, of potential and of hope of a future for the child, all of which seemed to us to be scattered like sands by the sea.

These emotions are experienced at various times. You might see a "neurotypical" child, younger than your child with autism, doing what yours cannot do, or see your child with autism struggling to do what comes almost naturally to another child. My inner state swung between calm and turmoil when I saw how other two-year olds were stringing words together, while my three-year-old son had no words and would not respond to any.

At other times, I worried if I was doing enough for Ade. What if I missed the most potent treatment and the best time for intervention has passed? I worried about the future for Ade. What would he be able to achieve? Would he get married or live an independent life? This often makes parents of a child with autism grieve all over again, and may make them isolate themselves, which again can lead to depression, and so the cyclical nature of the grief is once again set in motion.

For me, over the years, I found that I could refuse to be handcuffed by the limitation of this "cyclical grieving" by embracing my faith and by educating myself about autism.

THE QUEST FOR ANSWERS

When I finally began to come to my senses, I began to ask a hundred questions: What is autism? How did he get it? What is responsible? Why was it not detected during pregnancy? What is the impact of it on Ade? What kind of life would Ade live? Where do we go from here? What do I do now? My world was thrown into a state of confusion.

"Oh Lord, please help me and fix Ade," my heart cried out to my God (the One who gives children). I did not know what to do, but I knew I had to take the bull by the horns. My quest for answers turned me into a lifelong learner, starting with some of the materials that we were given by the paediatrician and the kind couple from the then Burgess Autistic Trust.

"Autism," according to the National Autistic Society, "is a lifelong developmental disability that affects how a person communicates with and relates to other people and how they experience the world around them" (autism.org.uk, 2020).

The NHS website (nhs.uk.2020) says that people with autism may :

- Find it hard to communicate and interact with other people.
- Find it hard to understand how other people think or feel.
- Find things like bright light or loud noises overwhelmingly stressful or uncomfortable.
- Take longer to understand information.
- Do or think the same things over and over.

The Holy book says that knowing the truth will set you free but knowing the fact of Ade's autism did not set me free. It invoked emotions too deep and too painful for expression. But I had to go on. The world does not stop for your grief; challenges are not stopped by your trauma. You must be courageous, brave and believe that there will be light at the end of the tunnel. No matter how long or how dark the tunnel may appear.

So, with faith in my heart and books in my hands, his dad and I continued our frantic search for answers. I read countless books, watched so many videos and even attended conferences, all in a bid to get answers, but none appeared to be forthcoming.

No one is sure of the true causes of autism. According to the National Autistic Society (NAS) "the causes of autism are still being investigated (autism.org.uk, 2020)." However, according to David.

G. Amaral, many experts believe that there may not be a single cause but instead various factors responsible for the pattern of behaviour that leads to the diagnosis of autism (Amaral, D. G. 2017).

There is intensive international effort aimed at understanding the causes and biology of autism, leading to earlier identification of and intervention to support autistic individuals, says Amaral (2007). According to the NHS, there are no cures or treatments for autism itself, although doctors may recommend medications and special diets for other conditions that affect individuals with autism or that are diagnosed as being on the autism spectrum (nhs.uk, 2019).

The Westminster Commission on Autism (2018) set up by the government (made up of a group of parliamentarians, people with autism, parents/carers, charities, academics and health professionals) has conducted a short inquiry into the regulation of treatments, therapies and products for people on the autism spectrum. In March 2018, the commission came out with its report: *A Spectrum of Harmful Intervention for Autism: A Short Report* (2018) which detailed a range of dangerous and unsubstantiated products and therapies that people with autism and their advocates had had offered or suggested to them. The Commission made recommendations for improved policy and practices to ensure that no person with autism is misled into using an unsubstantiated or even harmful product or therapy as an intervention for autism.

However, this is not to say that all interventions are useless or harmful. Dr Sarah Helps, a consultant clinical psychologist within the NHS noted that "There is a strong evidence base which points towards the fact that early intervention and proper support for children who may be suffering from autism and their families can help remediate the core deficits of autism and support families to feel more able to meet and manage their child's need" (Helps & Sheppard, N. 2015). It is therefore imperative that a parent does thorough research before embarking on any therapy for their child with autism. Hence my constant search for answers!

LESSONS LEARNT: After Ade was diagnosed with autism, I soon realised that I needed to come to grips with evidence-based information about autism. I believe that information gives power and knowledge gives hope. I believe adopting the following strategies were empowering in withstanding the flood of fear and sorrow unleashed by the diagnosis of autism:

- **GETTING KNOWLEDGEABLE ABOUT AUTISM**
  Through consuming as much evidence-based information as possible, hope rose within me, making me brave enough to take the steps to help Ade achieve his highest potential. The more I knew about autism, the better equipped I was to make informed decisions for Ade about the therapies and treatment options, the things to look out for and the kind of questions

to ask. That way, I became an active partner with the professionals in making treatment decisions for Ade, as I was fast becoming an expert by experience.

- **ATTENDING CONFERENCES AND NETWORKING**

  Other ways of becoming educated on autism, apart from reading, include going to autism conferences and networking with other parents who had been successful in their struggles with autism and improved the quality of life of their children. Conferences and workshops provide parents with the latest information on research, treatments and educational options, as well as a chance to meet and talk with other parents with the same concerns.

  These conferences expose one to effective programmes developed by outstanding researchers to help children with autism develop their communication, motor, academic and social skills, as well as opportunities for vocational training available to young adults with autism.

- **GETTING INVOLVED WITH SUPPORT GROUPS**

  Another way to get information and to cope with the stress of raising a child with autism is by networking with other similar families. These are often called support groups. These groups provided me with comfort in finding others who were experiencing similar situations. They allow parents to express their emotions openly and honestly, as well as to give and receive advice on the parenting process.

Such groups can also help tackle everyday situations like handling temper tantrums, toileting, sleep problems and family outings. They also provide resources on important transitions in life for your children, such as starting school, planning for college and work, independent living, and much more.

Members of these groups can also share information on the care services for your child and the role of the Local Education Authority. They can also tell you how you can get your child assessed for an Education, Health and Care Plan (EHC Plan), what private and public programmes are available in your area, where your child can get social skills training and whether speech, occupational, or physical therapy are recommended. Lastly, they can give you valuable information on what financial resources are available for you to access.

I am privileged to be part of three charities set up for families who have children with special educational needs and disabilities, and they have been of tremendous help to me. We have even travelled out of the country together as a group and the experience was phenomenal because no one was judging one another, and our children were comfortable in their own space. We also discuss issues that are common to our children and what we can do to make sure we continue to take care of ourselves physically, mentally, financially and emotionally.

- **GETTING RESPITE**

Research has shown that respite care is an important support in coping with the demands of raising a child with autism (Cooks, Smith & Brenner, 2020). Respite is a service in which another adult assumes the role of the parent for a child diagnosed with autism, giving the natural parents a break. This has been found to reduce stress levels in both parents. These services allow the parents to discuss current issues and to gain knowledge of their child's autism diagnosis.

- **BEING AWARE OF FALSE CLAIMS**

Given the uncertainty around autism, there are plenty of practitioners rushing to fill the vacuum with all sorts of ostensible cures. These therapies might even be popular, despite the warnings of medical and health professionals. Parents sometimes find themselves tempted by the allure of such alternative treatments promising relief or cure.

This is particularly appealing because people who are close to the family but who have little or no experience of autism may not always be the most sensitive. For example, they may find it difficult to tell the difference between a child with autism having a meltdown because of unexpressed and unmet needs, and a "neurotypical" child just being naughty. Some will even let you know how naughty they think your child is. This can be very frustrating for parents, who may then look to cure their child of these challenging behaviours at all costs.

Such treatments range from relatively benign interventions such as gluten-free diets or raw camels' milk to potentially dangerous ideas such as MMS (Miracle Master Mineral Solution). Some of these alternative treatments are not merely controversial, they come with costs that can extend beyond the financial and pose a threat to the physical and mental health of vulnerable families (Westminster Commission on Autism , 2018).

It is therefore vital that reliable information and advice is readily accessible to parents of children with autism, both after diagnosis and on an ongoing basis. For example, every Local Authority has a Local Offer website, which gives children and young people with special educational needs or disabilities and their families information about help and services in its local community. Similarly, the National Autistic Society's Autism Helpline offers confidential information, advice and support on everything to do with autism, and they are also able to signpost parents toward local sources of help and support (visit https://www.autism.org.uk/what-we-do/help-and-support).

- **FINDING OUT ABOUT SUPPORT AND HELP AVAILABLE**

Finally, the National Institute for Health and Care Excellence (NICE) in collaboration with the Social Care Institute for Excellence (SCIE) has published a guideline entitled "*Autism: the management and support of children and young people on the autism spectrum*" (NICE Clinical Guideline 170). This summarises the different ways professionals can provide support, treatment and help for children and young people with autism across the full range of intellectual abilities, from birth until their 19th birthday.

DEALING WITH THE CONUNDRUM

In the meantime, Ade continued to grow increasingly adorable. Trying to reconcile this adorable boy with the autism diagnosis left me feeling like my heart was completely shattered! The pain was excruciating as I thought that my dream of a bright future for Ade was being dashed by AUTISM!

I wondered how such a handsome boy would have to live his life in total silence, completely oblivious to the world around him. Like a tortoise, he had withdrawn to his shell. "Is this what autism does to people? What then does the future hold for him?" I wondered.

I pushed myself to the limit, challenging myself to believe the best, despite what was looking at me in the face. I kept asking myself whether he could have the future I wanted for him. It wasn't easy, but I decided that embracing hope was the only choice I had.

I tried my best to always keep hope alive, no matter how challenging the situation with Ade might be. In all these times, I wondered what other challenges we would have to face.

LESSONS LEARNT: Parenting is already an exhausting endeavour and taking care of a child with autism takes things to a whole new level of fatigue. Even when I have had a good night sleep or some time off, there was a level of emotional and physical tiredness and stress that was constantly present, which came simply from the weight of tending to the needs of the child with autism. Such stressors include:

- Ade's inability to express his basic needs. By the time Ade was diagnosed with autism, he had completely shut down.

- Attending therapies, as Ade often danced to his own tune, and did not see the need to follow demands made of him by the specialists.

- The need to constantly research new treatments and therapies available for autism because I was concerned about Ade's future welfare. Advocating for Ade in the educational, health and social care system was also a source of stress.

- The feeling of grief that sometimes permeated my mind over the loss of the "neurotypical" child I had been expecting or hoping for.

Although raising Ade challenged me and pushed me beyond what I thought were my limits, I also grew tremendously as a person. My faith helped me to start experiencing a sense of unexplainable joy, a sense of well-being, and a positive belief in Ade. Raising Ade also made me more reflective, more appreciative, more patient, and more empathetic toward others in a way I never would have been if I did not have Ade in my life.

This emotional shift was beautifully captured in the poem Welcome to Holland by Emily Perl Kingsley. Emily Perl Kingsley had a son whose disability was thought to be life-limiting, yet he experienced a successful and varied career. She therefore reminds me not to spend a lifetime mourning what might have been, but to look instead at setbacks and losses as opportunities for discovering something quite different, but perhaps also equally wonderful .

<u>Welcome To Holland</u>

by Emily Perl Kingsley

Copyright©1987 by Emily Perl Kingsley.

All rights reserved.

Reprinted by permission of the author.

I am often asked to describe the experience of raising a child with a disability - to try to help people who have not shared that unique experience to understand it, to imagine how it would feel. It's like this……

When you're going to have a baby, it's like planning a fabulous vacation trip - to Italy. You buy a bunch of guide books and make your wonderful plans. The Coliseum. The Michelangelo David. The gondolas in Venice. You may learn some handy phrases in Italian. It's all very exciting.

After months of eager anticipation, the day finally arrives. You pack your bags and off you go. Several hours later, the plane lands. The flight attendant comes in and says, "Welcome to Holland."

"Holland?!?" you say. "What do you mean Holland?? I signed up for Italy! I'm supposed to be in Italy. All my life I've dreamed of going to Italy."

But there's been a change in the flight plan. They've landed in Holland and there you must stay.

The important thing is that they haven't taken you to a horrible, disgusting, filthy place, full of pestilence, famine and disease. It's just a different place.

So you must go out and buy new guide books. And you must learn a whole new language. And you will meet a whole new group of people you would never have met.

It's just a different place. It's slower-paced than Italy, less flashy than Italy. But after you've been there for a while and you catch your breath, you look around.... and you begin to notice that Holland has windmills....and Holland has tulips. Holland even has Rembrandts.

But everyone you know is busy coming and going from Italy... and they're all bragging about what a wonderful time they had there. And for the rest of your life, you will say "Yes, that's where I was supposed to go. That's what I had planned."

And the pain of that will never, ever, ever, ever go away... because the loss of that dream is a very very significant loss.

But... if you spend your life mourning the fact that you didn't get to Italy, you may never be free to enjoy the very special, the very lovely things ... about Holland.

*   *   *

What a conundrum! I hated the sadness and helplessness I felt when Ade was diagnosed with autism, yet it was the sadness that led me to the place of total surrender needed to bring me to a place of appreciation, empathy and hope for a bright future for him. But even with this positivity, there are days I cannot help embracing sadness and anxiety when Ade wanders away from me to dance to a music of his own, I cannot appreciate.

THE TIP OF THE ICEBERG

Ade being diagnosed with autism didn't change him into another child, but the diagnosis seemed to set in stone the behavioural challenges Ade was experiencing. They weren't going to end or change, all were now fixed and final (or so I thought at the time). And that was heart-wrenching. Some of these behaviours would have been amusing if they didn't leave me feeling bewildered, exasperated or just flabbergasted.

For starters, imagine living with a child with no expressive language (the ability to use language to express oneself) and no receptive language (the ability to comprehend language). That was the case with Ade. He said nothing and seemed to understand nothing. So, no matter how many times we repeated a message to him, using the simplest of expressions or words, he made no response, no acknowledgement, just blankness. It was like all we had was Ade's body, while his mind had gone away somewhere unknown. It was a traumatising experience. I remember, we once visited a family friend and Ade positioned himself in front of their television set. Our friend wasn't amused, so he ordered Ade to move using a commanding voice, but Ade was completely unaware of what the man had said and stood unflustered where he was. The man was dazed. He remarked that Ade was the first child to flagrantly ignore his orders. His dad and I laughed, as if to say, "Welcome to our world!" But did Ade ignore our friend's command? Or did he lack conscious awareness of his environment? Or was it that he lacked receptive language? Only time would tell.

This apparent lack of reflective language also meant we were unsure what or even if Ade was learning from his environment and the educational resources he was constantly been exposed to. Despite these uncertainties, I made it a point of duty to read to him, to play games with him, to play him educational DVDs and CDs, and to take him to the library.

I have always believed that taking children to the library from a very young age helps instil in them a love of reading. Reading extends the imagination, frees the mind and prepares the child to stand on the greatest stages. I started taking Ade to the library when he was three months old, to read to him and to join in with the "baby boogies" (free music and rhyme activities organised by the library). All went well until Ade was about two and a half, when he seemed to have decided that he was no longer going to sit and participate in the activities, including "Storytime". While the other children sat by themselves or on their parent's laps to listen to stories, Ade was having none of that. Instead, he would be running around doing his own thing. If he eventually decided to join in, he would go straight to the librarian reading the story and try to take the storybook, as if to say it was his turn with the book. It wouldn't have felt so awful trying to defuse the situation, except I had over three dozen eyes giving me disapproving stares, wondering why I couldn't manage my child. Some people even dared to tell me to control my child. It seemed in their minds, Ade's behaviour was due to lack of discipline and I was simply a bad mother, end of story. If only it were that simple. But it is not simple, it is autism!

So, we stopped going to the library's activities for children. Instead, we started going when there were only a few people in the children's section. Even then I was always on high alert, as paying attention to a book meant taking an eye off Ade, which gave him the perfect opportunity to make a dash for the lift or run off to another part of the library, as if he did not get the memo that the library was meant to be a quiet space. So, I understand why many families affected by autism often feel shame, rejection and socially isolated, because I have lived the experience.

It did not end there, simply taking Ade to the park involved a plethora of emotions. "Why?" you might ask. Simple. One of Ade's favourite things to do at the park was to build sandcastles, and he occasionally threw sand into the air, oblivious to the other children in the vicinity. Sometimes the sand would find its way to a child's eyes, resulting in screams, stares and shouts. Screams from the affected child, intense stares from onlookers and distressing shouts from the affected parents. "'I'm very sorry," I'd say, determined to keep yet a closer watch over Ade, who would joyously continue building his castle, completely unaware of the impact he was making.

When he was satisfied with the sandcastle he had built, he went hopping from one play equipment to the other, which is part of what going to the park is all about. Other times, however, he found it thrilling to suddenly run towards the park's entrance, sending waves of fear up my spine as I scrambled to my feet to dash after him. He is quite light on his feet and I couldn't afford to have him out of my sight when out and about. This was exhausting, not least because the path to the park's entrance was uphill! So, going to the park for Ade was a wonderful time full of thrills and spills, where I had to play the secret intelligence agent, anticipating Ade's every move to prevent him rocking the boat and creating drama.

Talking about drama, I will never forget the day Ade refused to leave the park when I let him know it was time to go home. This happened when Ade was three years old. We had been in the park for quite a while and I announced that it was time to go home (even though Ade was non-verbal we were encouraged to speak to him). He simply refused, buckling his knees under him and falling on the soft green grass. As was so often the case, I wondered whether his refusal was because he couldn't or wouldn't obey. I simply didn't know. All I knew was my persistent pleading was falling on deaf ears and I was at my wits end as to what to do. I could have tried to pick him up into my arms, except I also had to be mindful of his sister, who was four at the time. As I was still wondering what to do, a kind gentleman who had come to walk his dog came over curious as to what was going on, seeing Ade lying almost motionless on the green grass and me standing beside him trying to pull him up to no avail.

The gentleman asked what was going on, and I explained the situation to him. He said he would help as my child was clearly a handful. He explained the strategy he had in mind to get Ade home. At the count of four, he said, we would lift Ade, take four steps counting, stop, count up to four, lift him again, and we would repeat the whole process until we got Ade home. The idea was very welcoming, this way, the gentleman could use his free hand to hold his dog and I could use mine to hold my daughter. This method was magical, Ade enjoyed it so much that after the third stop, he stopped resisting and started anticipating the next lift. That was how we got him home. Honestly, I don't know how I would have gotten Ade home on my own. Thankfully, we got home with no more resistance and without me having to tear my hair out. I was grateful to the gentleman and, to me, he was an angel in disguise for I never saw him again, not even in the park.

Going on buses was also an interesting experience, to say the least. For Ade, the bus's bell was a delight, as a result, he would reach out his hand and press the bell even if we hadn't got to our stop, making the bus driver pull over when no one was getting off. This was funny to Ade but not to the bus driver, not to the passengers and not to me, who had to say sorry a thousand times in the various buses we took. The passengers also sometimes let me know that I needed to control Ade better. Ade was oblivious of the impact his little game was having on the other passengers, other than the fact that his mum started keeping him away far from any seat with a bell pole.

One might think that with the thrill Ade get from pressing buses' bells he wouldn't mind loud noises, but Ade was highly sensitive to them. As a family, we tried our best to avoid loud and crowded places. We often had to leave shops, museums and social functions when it became too overwhelming and Ade couldn't bear it anymore. We have had to leave social functions almost as soon as we got there because Ade would be upset and crying. I remember once when Ade was about four and a half, we went to a party. As soon as we walked into the hall, Ade became visibly distressed, putting his hands in his ears, screaming and trying to pull away to try and get out of the building. His dad decided to take him out of the hall and later told me that as soon as Ade was out of that hall, he was calm and played happily in the park.

Ade found the whole experience of shopping extremely overwhelming and traumatising, with everything that goes on in a shopping centre. The busy crowds, the bright lighting, the loud noises and all the items arranged in the shop were causing him sensory overload. So, when going shopping with him, we stayed for only as long as necessary and tried to pay before Ade started screaming and throwing tantrums. Ade often attracted disapproving stares and a few words to the effect that he needed to be better controlled. Although some people seemed very empathetic to us, as if to say, "We understand, keep pushing on!" This was always like an oasis in the desert. Very refreshing!

It is, however, quite puzzling that the same Ade who doesn't like the hustle and bustle of the shopping mall, somehow managed to be fascinated by its escalators, and especially their big red emergency stop buttons. You should see the kind of disapproving stares we got from people who had to take the stairs whilst some engineer tried to get the escalator going. It was always a distressing scene. I became hyper-alert whenever we were approaching an escalator and would run to where the stop button was and cover it with my foot until Ade had gone past. Only then could I relax and sigh in relief.

But I shouldn't have been surprised that Ade was fascinated by these things. After all, switches and locks have held him spellbound all his life. I remember he was barely three years old when he figured out the safety locks and the safety gate's locking mechanism. We soon realised that to keep Ade out of a room, the door had to be locked and the keys removed. Child safety locks didn't deter Ade from getting into anything. Once, when I enrolled for a course and Ade attended the creche provided, one of the things the ladies at the creche were keen to tell me when I went to collect him, was that Ade had done something no other child had ever done in the twenty-five years of the creche's existence. When I asked them what that was, they said he had managed to open a cabinet that no child had ever once managed to open! I smiled sheepishly, thinking that was so typical of Ade.

Ade's uniqueness was written all over the things he did, wherever he went. For example, when he started nursery, we were constantly told that he wasn't joining in with circle time, or indeed at any other times. While other children were enjoying colouring, finger painting, sensory play, sorting colours, singing and dancing to nursery rhymes, Ade just liked to be by himself playing with cars, books or Lego. When another child came to play alongside him, Ade abandoned whatever he was playing with and moved to another place where he could be alone. His dad and I were keenly aware the Ade seemed to be pulled by invisible hands towards solitude. When he was three years old, my childhood friend came from abroad with her children (who were the same age as Ade) to spend a week with us. Ade ignored them completely. It was as if they were not even there as he continued to seek his own company.

But Ade could not be described as a shy boy. Rather, he seemed largely oblivious to the people around him and simply preferred to avoid them. He always drifted towards solitary spaces or the corners of a room, whether at home, at the nursery and even in social places.

When we were visiting friends (which we did less and less because of all the interesting behaviours that come with autism), I was always getting up to bring Ade back to where the rest of us were, otherwise he would do his own house viewing, going from room to room trying to find the most solitary corner.

Sometimes, friends would try to calm me down by saying, "Don't worry, come and sit down, let him be in his own space." But that was exactly the opposite of what we believed was good for Ade. We wanted him to learn to spend time around other people, children and adult alike, with the belief that in time he would learn and develop the social skills he needed to build and maintain friendships and grow towards independence and a fruitful life.

However, when Ade was alone, his favourite things to do were to line up his cars, stare into books or play with his Lego. When he was playing with Lego, he had to complete sets. He would get distressed if any parts were missing and couldn't just use an alternate piece. At age four, Ade developed an interest in SpongeBob and its soft toys. These soft toys lived (and live) on Ade's bed and he will not sleep until all of them are there. Once, he went out with them to his aunt's place and thought he'd left one of them behind. When I put Ade to bed, he realised "Plankton", one of his SpongeBob characters, was missing and he started screaming, got up and went straight for the front door as if to say, "Go and get Plankton." I immediately called his aunt to check if Ade had left Plankton in her place whilst we searched our entire house. She called back to say it wasn't at her place. After an hour of non-stop searching, with Ade all the while wailing and reaching for the door, I finally found it tucked away inside Ade's duvet, I was as overjoyed as if I had had a million-pound jackpot. You should have seen Ade's face when he saw Plankton. He beamed from ear to ear. With great joy, Ade climbed onto his bed and fell soundly asleep a few minutes later, as if all had just been a dream. In his sleep, he looked so adorable, making the search worth the while!

The behaviour attributed to autism that I find most intriguing is the difficulty children diagnosed with autism have in making or maintaining eye contact. The Speech and Language Therapist alerted us to the fact that Ade had fleeting eye contact and that good eye contact was very important for normal social interaction, as looking at people helps children get more information about language based on their observation of facial expressions, signs and gestures. She therefore recommended several ways for us to encourage him to look at us more, including playing some games with him. I struggled with this advice as a result of a culture clash. What do I mean? I am a British Nigerian. In Nigeria, as in many African cultures, it is considered a sign of respect to avoid eye contact or to have sporadic or brief eye contact at most. It is seen as impudent for children and young people to look into the eyes of older people during a conversation (Mbele, J. 2011). On the other hand, maintaining constant eye contact in the white British culture is considered polite and proper, a sign of sincerity, interest and self-confidence. Consequently, anyone who makes little or fleeting eye contact is seen as rude, deceitful or up to no good (Roger, W.S. 2011). Here was my dilemma, if I encouraged Ade to maintain constant eye contact in line with the Western culture, he would be seen as rude, aggressive and uncultured by the Nigerian elders, and if I taught him to adopt fleeting eye contact, he would be seen as rude, deceitful and lacking in confidence by Westerners!

LESSONS LEARNT: As a parent, you need to develop thick skin, fast. When I go out in public with Ade, I try to manage the unpredictability of Ade's behaviour, his distress (for example, Ade does not like loud noises) and the responses of others present (such as stares and comments). This kind of emotional intelligence is often displayed by parents with children with autism. We keep our poise, rather than expressing our feelings about the responses of others towards our children or ourselves. This can leave the general public unaware of the emotional turmoil we experience.

Similarly, given the lack of outward signs of autism, when the child unwittingly breaks social rules by refusing or ignoring requests, being aggressive or throwing tantrums, engaging in self-stimulatory behaviour like rocking or hand-flapping, eating or mouthing non-edible items, hurting themselves or others by biting or hitting, or simply running off, parents often appear to be incompetent parents, rather than as parents of children with particular social and communication disorders (Ryan, s. 2010).

This often leaves parents, including me, with the physically exhausting and emotionally draining responsibility of not only managing the unpredictability of a child's behaviour but also dealing with the judgments (consciously or unconsciously) passed by others through their stares or comments. For example, once Ade went missing at a social gathering and after looking for him for a while, we found him in one of the rooms attached to the main hall where we were all gathered. I thanked all the people there, and one woman said to my face, "I didn't help look for him because if you were firmer with him, he wouldn't have gone missing." This felt like a slap in the face. (It was in the early days when we were still going from one specialist to another trying to learn what was wrong with Ade.) Worse still, this experience is not unique to me, and neither was it the last time I experienced it. This type of response from others often leaves one feeling like a bad parent with poor parenting skills, even after having autism diagnosed.

The intense distress public places can create for children with autism, the lack of understanding often displayed by other people, and the emotional turbulence this creates, all combine to mean that parents often keep children with autism out of public spaces. This is a cause for concern, as it deprives children with autism of the opportunity for the social interaction they need, isolates parents and other family members, and prevents society at large from gaining an understanding of autism.

One way some parents act to stave off this kind of judgment by others is by disclosing the child's autism, either verbally or through the use of badges, labelled t-shirts, or even handing out cards from the National Autistic Society (autism.org.uk) to let people know your child has autism and that he might need more time or help in certain situations. However, disclosure is not always practical in public settings where there is a constant flow of people.

I, however, do not feel particularly comfortable using the label of autism in front of Ade, as I have come to appreciate that a lot of Ade's actions are not illogical, they are just different, apparently driven by different goals, different priorities, and different ways of relating to the world from those of the majority.

There is a need to raise greater awareness of the emotional complexity of public encounters experienced by parents of children with autism and for a greater understanding of the behaviour of children diagnosed with autism so there can be more tolerance for their unusual behaviours in public places.

Often, a child diagnosed with autism displaying challenging behaviour is not being naughty but is experiencing sensory issues in response to a wide range of stimuli. Looking back, I realised that the many moments that Ade had where he couldn't sit still, where he kept putting his hands in his ears, where he lifted his voice in high screams, where I had to piggyback him throughout an outing because he was aiming for the doors, these weren't Ade being naughty but were down to sensory issues. Ade was hyper-sensitive to the sounds, sights, touches, tastes and smells around him. Apart from these well-known five senses, it is also known that children diagnosed with autism may also be affected by two additional senses: the vestibular sense (the sense of movement and balance located in the inner ear) and the proprioceptive sense (the sense of body awareness in space located in our muscles and joints) (autismtas.org.au 2020), and these also often make them uncomfortable. This kind of sensory overload can make such children shut down or have a complete meltdown. As Bill Nason wisely observed "an autistic person's sensory experience of the world can have a profound effect on their life. "Parents, caregivers and teachers need to be aware that sensory processing issues can be one of the biggest challenges people on the spectrum experience (Nasen, B. 2014)."

Moreover, considering the culture clash I experienced with eye contact, I believe the relevance of culture to autism is significant, especially when interpreting the behaviours that constitute the baseline for diagnosing autism and society's responses to that behaviour. It is important for professionals to be familiar with the norms and values of the different families they are supporting, as what may be culturally accepted to one culture may be frowned at in another culture - maintaining constant eye contact for example. Remember, most widely used tests for autism are based on Western cultural norms, and parents and carers from non-western cultures may have different expectations of how children should behave (Derweerdt, S. 2012) .

PLEASE CALL THE POLICE TO FIND THE ADVENTURER

It is difficult to explain how I felt the first time I realised Ade was missing. It was as if my entire world had collapsed, leaving me in a state of emotional trauma, and the ensuing pandemonium made my head spin. For a long time after the diagnosis, we were involved with the police, not for any crime committed by his dad and I, but because of a son who loved to **WANDER!**

I searched everywhere, even under the tiniest objects, as if by some unexplainable phenomenon he could hide there. It was overwhelming. When all our efforts proved futile, we had no choice but to call the police.

At first, Ade's escapes made no sense and we thought he was just wandering off, but as he got older, he was able to give us a logical explanation. Once, he decided he needed to go to the store to get some SpongeBob toys, another time he decided he had to see the people who taxied him to school, yet another time, to visit a friend's house. "All doors must be bolted and checked," said the understanding men in uniform.

Yes, we kept the door bolted and checked but we couldn't keep Ade indoors forever. How can I ever forget waiting for a whole HOUR whilst the security personnel in LEGOLAND searched for Ade?

That day began with a lot of excitement. We were going to LEGOLAND in a coach with some other families with children and young people with special needs. The coach was alive with music and laughter. The children couldn't hide their excitement, despite the hitches on the way. For example, when the coach was misdirected by the satnav to take a road that was too narrow for it to travel, the children stayed unusually calm while we all waited for the coach to manoeuvre back to the main road. It was so interesting seeing the children empowered to calm themselves by the thoughts of going on rides at the LEGOLAND. There were so much joy and laughter in the coach as we made our way to the park!

When we finally arrived at LEGOLAND, we all alighted. Within a seeming instant Ade had vanished! The joy that had saturated the coach was replaced by fierce, piercing claws of fear grabbing my heart. Time ceased for a moment. I had to rise above it. I chose not to surrender to fear. I chose not to panic. Courage and bravery propelled my feet forward and let me ask my fellow passengers if, by chance, they had seen Ade. "No!" went each one. "Don't worry we'll find him." I heard the voices of the passengers as if at a distance as my mind tried hard to focus on what to do next.

"Who to ask now?" I thought as I took hold of my daughter's hand and ran to the security at the park entrance. "Please, did you see a boy wearing a green top and khaki trousers wandering around by himself?" I asked, as calmly as I could, given the billion directions my mind was racing in.

"Oh, no, we haven't," replied the concerned guard. Knowing that time was of the essence, the security personnel radioed all their colleagues in the car park if they had seen a boy wandering about, but it was no use!

"We'll do our best to find your son," declared the head of the security department as she led us to a waiting room while they combed the whole massive area of land that LEGOLAND occupies. It was like looking for a needle in a haystack.

I had to remain extremely calm as all this was going on. I stayed calm, even though I knew staying calm held no magic, even though I knew staying calm did not necessarily make my situation any better. But I still chose to stay calm, because I was determined not to ruin the fun for the other families who had come with us to take advantage of the day. The day when the birds were chirping happily, when flowers were blooming in full array and people were enjoying the warm summer sun - a glorious day to be in the park to explore and to share laughter. No, I would not mar the joy of others on such a lovely day.

Still today, many of those families are still amazed by my calmness. They found it incredible! But I had told myself that there was no point indulging in theatrics, as becoming hysterical at that point would not help to find Ade. After all, I have always believed that the world does not stop for one's grief. I knew that some of those parents did not understand me and never would.

So, I continued to offer silent prayers as I sat waiting to hear whether Ade has been found. It was one of the longest hours of my life. I had come to the park with two kids and I just had to believe that I would leave the park with the two kids. It was not easy at all, but I had to summon all the faith I had.

"Oh!" went the security guard. It had just occurred to him to ask my daughter for the ride she thought her brother might be interested in going on. Without hesitation, she said it had to be the "desert chase and thunder blazer", as she had seen him checking out the ride on the family's iPad as soon as he learnt we were visiting LEGOLAND. Boom! He got the security personnel for that ride on the radio and gave them Ade's description. "He's with you!" I heard the security guard exclaim. When he dropped the radio, he smiled and said, "Your son has been found and they're bringing him!"

My joy knew no bounds as relief swept over me. Have you ever waited for something; your whole body electrified by the power of anticipation? That was how I felt, which made waiting for Ade's arrival a tormenting experience. The wait was simply interminable! Finally, Ade was brought into the room and when I saw him, I was moved with the love that came over me the first time I held him in my hands. I held him so tight in my arms and I did not want to let him go.

When I finally released him, he looked at me. He had no inkling of the ordeal he had just put me through. I couldn't help smiling and I thanked the kind team of security personnel who had been extremely supportive and effective in helping me find Ade. We exited the room and I took my children on various rides, determined that the children and I were going to have a great time despite the earlier drama.

Some may think it strange that I was able to carry on after the emotional trauma I had just endured but for me carrying on was the only way to stay strong. After all, bringing up a son diagnosed with autism means I have learnt to manage my emotions and find the strength to carry on even during the most chaotic situations. The show must go on! We had a wonderful time at the park and went home exhausted.

However, that was not the end of Ade's explorations. His desire for adventure was so strong that he even got away from his school and they also had to get the police involved. The school said that they were particularly worried because the road right in front of his school was such a busy one that they feared he might come to serious harm. Thank goodness, the police responded swiftly, and he was returned to the school unharmed. On and on went the apologies from his school management when they informed us of the incident at the close of the day. You could see a wave of relief wash over their faces when we told them we understood and did not plan to press any charges. There was no point playing the hypocrite, after all he had wandered away even from our sight. They, however, promised to put stricter safety measures in place so that such an incident would never repeat itself. True to their word, it never did.

For a long time to come, we (his parents) remained on high alert, as Ade was resolute that there were still journeys he had to embark on alone, and heaven forbid if his agenda was not quickly detected! It was as if he had heard the call from the INVICTUS poem (particularly the last stanza) by Williams Ernest Henley (Invictus, 2020):

"*It matters not how strait the gate,*

How charged with punishments the scroll,

I am the master of my fate,

I am the captain of my soul."

Such was the anxiety that became our companion that whenever I now see a poster displaying a missing person, I stop and say a prayer that they will soon be found, knowing the troubled souls of those searching will only find solace in the safe return of their loved one!

LESSON LEARNT: So puzzling was Ade's wandering that I needed to find some answers to soothe my wondering mind. It was interesting to read that children with autism frequently wander under any kind of supervision, and it is often a form of communication where the child is expressing a need or desire, or a refusal. They wander either to get to something interesting or away from something challenging (nationalautismassociation.org. 2020).

I recently came across an article entitled Autism Plus Wandering by Beth Arky (2018), which states:

"According to the responses from more than 800 parents, roughly 50 percent of children between the ages of 4 and 10 with an ASD wander at some point, four times more than their unaffected siblings. The behaviour peaks at 4, but almost 30 percent of kids with an ASD between the ages of 7 and 10 are

still eloping, eight times more than their unaffected brothers and sister (Arky, B. 2018)."

Although, it is good to know that there are many more parents in the same boat as us, apprehension and terror of having a child run like Usain Bolt is something no parent should experience!

Fortunately, the American Academy of Paediatrics (Hyman, S. & McIIwain, 2019) have suggested a number of things that parents can do to prevent or at least reduce the chances of children with autism wandering. These include:

- Shutting and locking all doors that lead outside the home, irrespective of the child's age.
- Teaching the child communication and behaviour strategies that help deal with challenging circumstances instead of running away. Teachers and other people involved in the care of the child should also be aware of child's tendency to wander when stressed.
- Being aware of the things that may trigger wandering for the child. These may be places they love to run to (such as the park) or situations they find stressful that may make them run away (like loud noises).

- Consider using monitoring technology and identification tags on the child, as one third of children with autism are unable to communicate basic details about themselves.

- Communicating the rules you expect your child to follow when out and about and staying alert.

- Establishing a sleep routine for the child, as a lack of sleep can make them hyperactive. Where a child with autism is having sleep problems, consult the paediatrician for assessment and necessary intervention. Parents and carers also need to get enough rest to help stay vigilant.

AMAZING GRACE

No doubt there is a supreme being who watches over us, how else to explain how Ade has survived all his escapades? As if his wandering was not troubling enough, there was no part of the house that was too high for Ade to climb. His grandmother nicknamed him "Adegoke" (one who has come to climb great heights). One day, we even found him with one foot on the window in the bathroom on the first floor trying to climb down and you can only imagine how vigorously we quaked in our shoes!

I kept thinking about what would have happened if we had not arrived in the nick of time, as it was on the first floor of the building. Hopefully, it would not have been the end of him but how many bones would he have broken? So frightening were these thoughts that we decided not only must the doors be locked, the windows must be under lock and key as well.

For Ade, however, doors and windows were gateways to adventure, and even household objects were worth exploring. I remember one day I came into the kitchen and I saw Ade drenched from head to toe in oil, having taken a two-litre bottle of cooking oil and decided to anoint himself. It was such a remarkable sight - I didn't know whether to laugh or to cry as Ade tried to use his hands to rub the oil off his body. Fortunately, my older sister came in at this time, burst into laughter and encouraged me to take him for a bath while she cleared up the mess.

How can I ever forget having to keep the shampoo and the body cream away because, for Ade, there was boundless joy in mixing them and trying to have a taste of them? He also loved to mix different sauces, as well as different ingredients, so much so that by age three he was trying to bake a cake unaided. When I tried to prevent him, my older sister in her wisdom, sat down with him while he mixed the ingredients and at the age of three, Ade made his first cake.

Someone familiar with autism will know that some children with autism may have "pica". According to the National Autistic Society, pica is the eating or mouthing non-edible items, such as stones, dirt and metal. It is believed that causes of pica in a person with autism may be medical, sensory, dietary or behavioural, including not understanding which items are edible and inedible. It may be a way of relieving anxiety or stress, feeling the taste or texture of the item, avoiding demands or just seeking attention (Shea et al, 2019).

For the professionals, all these reasons may explain or even justify this behaviour but for a parent, it is a scary situation. To have to keep an eye on your child 24/7 to prevent them from putting dangerous things in their mouth is exhausting and mentally stressful. When I think about how far Ade has come with regards to these issues, I become emotional and extremely thankful. I can't help thinking of the words of the hymn Amazing Grace by John Newton, particularly the verse that says:

"Through many dangers, toils and snares, I have already come; 'Tis grace has brought me safe thus far And grace will lead me home." (Newton, J. 1779)

LESSON LEARNT: Thoughts and logic have limits and can only take a person so far. Many times, I had come to the end of my strength and without the grace of God, neither Ade nor I would have made it through. I am aware that religion is not everyone's cup of tea, but for me, my faith in God and His commitment to me has been my bedrock. I depend on God for strength and grace to carry on daily.

When I consider all the dangers Ade has passed through unharmed, I am more convinced that a great God is watching over us!

When Ade was diagnosed with autism, I felt a deep sense of grief and emptiness. I was determined that it would not become a life-long burden to bear, yet I could not overcome the cloud of sorrow that had descended over me.

It was my faith in God that shielded my heart from being pierced by the fiery dart thrown at me by the challenges of autism and the fear and grief that were swirling around for long after the diagnosis.

When I find no rhyme or rhythm to keep my mind at equilibrium it is in God that my heart finds stability, believing that something good can come if I give my all to God. This experience has increased my spiritual connectedness and has given me the strength and courage to deal with the challenges and emotional stress involved with raising Ade and to grow through it.

I know with God on my side, I will continue in the journey to help Ade maximise his potential and to live a happy, fruitful and healthy life. Whether that means I will find the courage to bear the challenges or that Ade will improve I do not yet know.

If there no way to solve the puzzles autism has set me, I find comfort in God. It was not that I had it all figured out but that

I knew that by God's grace Ade was going to be alright, even when he had become completely non-verbal and seemed oblivious to the world. I had peace in my heart because I was sure that God loved Ade much more than I do. After all, we are all God's children and in Him, we live, we move, and we find ourselves.

Over the years, I have seen events in Ade's life that could only be described as miracles and the direct intervention of a divine God. For instance, Ade's desire for adventure has taken him onto several busy roads with their attendant danger, yet he has always been found unharmed. What about the time he chose to climb so high and he was caught in the nick of time? Was that a coincidence? I do not believe so. I believe God in whose care I had placed Ade sent us to him before he jumped.

I know the journey ahead is still long, but progress is assured, whatever we may face and wherever the road may lead, because God's help is ever with us. Through God's grace, whatever happens, Ade will live a long, fruitful and fulfilling life!

FREED AT LAST!

Life is full of twist and turns. When I felt like I was in troubled waters, with crushing torrents of hopelessness and helplessness, unpredicted events gently stabled the boat. "That's amazing!" I exclaimed as an uncle told us how his son (the same age as Ade) had been born with a tongue-tie (ankyloglossia) and had had it snipped free.

I was excited because Ade was also tongue-tied. I went again to my new GP, as earlier ones had declined to recognise it as a problem. I hoped it might give Ade a chance to speak again (maybe, or maybe not, we would never know unless the procedure was carried out).

After Ade's birth, the paediatrician had said that his tongue-tie was only moderate, so all that might be affected was his ability to lick ice cream. Another GP said it didn't matter, while another GP considered cutting it unnecessary, likening it to cutting a big belly button. That was how five years of Ade's life rolled by. Somehow, I had to believe that this time was going to be different, and I was right!

As soon as I expressed my desire to have Ade's tongue freed, my new GP made the necessary referral without any hesitation. As if in a trance, before two weeks were over, the specialist had contacted us.

When we met with the specialist, her first comment to us was, "Why did you wait this long?" We explained our experiences up to that point and she could only empathise with our plight.

Shortly after our first meeting with the specialist, we were given a date for the simple surgical procedure called a "frenotomy" to release his tongue. The day finally came and under local anaesthetic, Ade's tongue was freed. I often wonder what would have happened if I had given up after having been denied three times!

After the procedure, something very special began to happen in our household. Could this be real?

> LESSON LEARNT: It is important for parents to trust their instincts and to persist based on the school of thought they believe will best serve their child. To cut or not to cut a tongue-tie is a hot topic of debate, with professionals on opposing sides of the issue. Some professionals (dentists and medical doctors) recommend that children with speech delays who are tongue-tied should have it the procedure to help their speech improve and to prevent potential speech difficulties in the future.

For example, *Speech and Feeding Improvements in Children After Posterior Tongue-Tie Release: A Case Series*, an article published in 2018 written in an International Journal of Clinical Paediatrics alluded to Frenectomy (cutting/clipping of tongue-tie) describes frenectomy as a low-risk procedure that can allow for functional improvement in speech intelligibility, sound acquisition, and feeding success (Baaxter, R. & Hughes, L. 2018).

On the other side of the argument are the professionals who see no correlation between a tongue-tie and speech delays. For example, a report by NHS Bedfordshire Community Health Service says: *"tongue-tie does not necessarily cause speech problems, but difficulty with the co-ordination of tongue movements can cause unclear speech, especially when children start putting words together in sentences. Difficulty with 'l' is also common. However, there is no direct link between the severity of a tongue tie and speech difficulties and any such problems may be for other reasons"* (*childspeechbedfordshire.nhs.uK. 2020*).

At the end of the day, it is for parents to decide what they believe is best for their child, as well-meaning doctors may underestimate the problems or may not believe there is a connection between a tongue-tie and the child's speech problems. We believe that having Ade's tongue freed helped him in developing his speech further. We had to persist but fortunately it turned out to be right for Ade!

APPLES OF GOLD IN PICTURES OF SILVER

Wait a moment. Was I hearing correctly? I heard Ade begin to read words from books, even though at this stage, he was yet to say anything to anyone. Soon, bit by bit, his words started coming. He started communicating with us and, remarkably, he started responding to his name and to requests. It was like he had listened enough and had decided it was finally his turn to be heard.

As I pondered how having Ade's tongue freed had contributed to his talking once again, I realised that it is important never to lose heart. No matter the ugliness and disappointment one may have faced, unimaginable beauty and pleasant surprises may just be around the corner!

Oh, what joy! Ade was finally becoming an active member of our family. Each word he spoke was music to my ears and a delight to my heart. To finally hear Ade, say Hallelujah! was the icing on the cake. I had held on to the belief that the day he said Hallelujah! would end my inner debate about whether he would ever develop functional language. As the Bible has it: every word was fitly spoken, like apples of gold in pictures of silver. Thank God, that day finally came!

The way he began to talk and the words he used reminded me of the toddler book Penguin by Polly Dunbar (2007). In that book, a boy called Ben is pleased when he opens his present and finds a penguin inside. Ben says "Hello!" to Penguin but Penguin says nothing. Ben pulls his funniest face, does a dizzy dance, sings a silly song, tickles Penguin and puts on a happy hat but Penguin says nothing. Ben asks, "Can't you talk?" yet Penguin says nothing. However, when a passing lion intervenes Penguin says everything!

When Ade began to talk, he talked a lot, and more than talking, he was curious about the world and asked countless questions. One sure way to know Ade was awake was when you started to hear: "WHY?" Tiring but also very exciting!

LESSONS LEARNT: When Ade was still living in his own distant world, not speaking nor responding to words, his grandma said, "Let him be, you can't put words in his mouth. When he is ready, he will speak." That was pretty much what happened, except I learnt along the way that there are some things that one can do to encourage language in a child with autism. For example, I learnt that:

- When I engaged Ade in games he enjoys, it encouraged his social interactions.

- I needed to continue to talk with Ade even if he did not respond, especially using what motivates him, as this encouraged him to learn to communicate.

- Mimicking Ade's behaviour and accompanying his actions with words was helpful in inspiring him to be more vocal and interactive.

- I needed to call Ade's name before I started talking to him (which I still try to do now), and not to start talking to him until I was sure he was paying attention to me.

- I needed to use language simple enough for him to understand at his developmental level.

- I should utilise body language when talking with Ade and where possible.

- I should provide him with technological aids and visual support.

- I needed to create situations that would prompt Ade to use his language communicatively, for example waiting for him to ask instead of me rushing to do things for him. After all, a mother is a person who can hear a child without a word being uttered!

More importantly, I learnt that believing that Ade was competent was the most crucial thing I could do to encourage him, whether he became verbal or remained non-verbal. It was the greatest way of empowering him.

OFF TO SCHOOL

The future seemed to be coming alive, bringing fresh hope as Ade started making progress against all odds! After having Portage play sessions at home, he attended a fantastic special resort centre called Phoenix Pre-School Centre. The Centre provides early identification and intervention, assessment and transition support for children with special educational needs or a disability. It offers access to a wide range of coordinated, multi-agency support and services. Ade loved it there, and he began to break out of his cocoon.

While Ade was at the Centre, his teachers often asked us what motivated him, as he did not seem moved by the usual things like a promise of a treat or the threat of a withdrawal of a beloved toy. We told them we found him the same at home and the usual rewards and consequences didn't work with Ade. Instead, we had learnt to stay calm no matter the situation and acted like broken records, making the same demand gently over and over while Ade decided whether or not he was going to comply. It was so difficult figuring out whether his refusals were "CAN'T DO IT" or "WON'T DO IT" that we had to learn to be flexible and collaborate with him.

Collaboration was the approach the teachers adopted at school as they worked around what he was able to do, and helped him develop the skills he needed, whether they were academic or more general skills such as social skills. The teachers at the centre were simply fantastic but after a year he had to leave the cosy nest and start reception in the big school.

Few months before Ade turned five, he started reception with his peers. His first day going into his reception class in primary school was emotional. It had been a long journey full of so many difficulties and now Ade was going into school with a language to communicate with and with the ability to respond. It was so surreal that I could not help being been grateful for how far Ade had come. As Alexandre Dumas said: "*He who has felt the deepest grief is able to experience supreme happiness.*"

Ade was loved by his teacher and she was keen to bring out the best in him. This made us incredibly happy despite his teacher's assertion that, "although he was the most adorable, he was the most challenging, as he liked to push the boundaries." Telling us that he liked to push the boundaries was preaching to the choir. We were keenly aware of this as it was our daily reality!

Not only did he push boundaries, he did his best to resist and avoid the ordinary demands of life. Dr Phil Christie, a Consultant Child

Psychologist remarked that the avoidance behaviour was an anxiety-driven need to be in control and to avoid other people's demands and expectations. Although Dr Phil Christie could explain why Ade avoided demands, it did not make it less frustrating for us as adults with the responsibility of educating him. However, the fact that he was thriving at school despite all these challenges was enough to fill our hearts with joy and hope.

For the first time, Ade had a friend. His friend Mark (not his real name) was non-verbal but Ade liked him. When Ade got home from school, he talked non-stop about Mark and the mischief Mark got into. Ade would giggle about it all. This ritual went on almost every school day.

It was so pleasurable watching Ade making friends and settling into the routine of school without fuss. This was how I hoped his time at school and education was going to continue, as there finally appeared to be a calm after the storm.

LESSONS LEARNT: One of the biggest decisions that parents of a child with autism will have to make is deciding the type of school the child will attend. In making this decision, the child's individual needs should always be the starting point rather than what would suit the parents' egos or what others might think. For instance, is the school somewhere the child will be happy, secure and able to reach his full potential?

As Ade's parents, his dad and I were best placed to decide on his school because we knew him better than anyone, yet we knew we would be foolish not to ask for help in arriving at this decision, so we sought the views of the professionals that had previously been involved with him, such as the educational psychologist, the speech and language therapist and the inclusion support professionals.

The school placement options available for Ade included mainstream schools, special schools and specialist units or resourced provisions. Some were separate institutions; others were part of mainstream schools. Some of the units were specifically for children with autism. There were also options of a residential school or home education.

A local authority is obliged to secure an Education, Health and Care plan (EHC Plan) in consultation with the parents. Mainstream or special state schools, and independent special schools, must, in theory, admit a child with autism unless the governing body or the Local Education Authority thinks doing so would be unsuitable (see section 38(3) of the Children and Families Act 2014)). As Ade already had an EHC Plan (then known as a Statement of Special Educational

Needs), we had a legal right to request a particular school (or to express a preference for an independent school).

When we went visiting the schools we were considering for Ade, we met up with the teachers and support staff to discuss his needs. The things we looked out for were:

- The depth of the school staff's knowledge of autism.

- The resources and strategies they would have to help him.

- Access Ade would have to other professionals, such as a therapist.

- The ability of the staff to support Ade's needs.

- Collaboration between school, other professionals and parents.

- Their approach to home-school communication.

- Whether Ade would have access to either a full, reduced or modified curriculum.

- Opportunities Ade would have for socialising with children who have similar needs and if he would also be mixing with "neurotypical" children.

- Their bullying policy and prevention strategies.

Having considered all these, we decided to send Ade to a specialist unit specifically for children with autism that was part of a mainstream school. Even though it was a bit of a drive from home, we knew Ade could manage the journey - but the commute wasn't to be the problem!

EDUCATIONAL ISSUES

Oh no! What a great error our decision to move Ade to another school in Year 2 when he was seven years old, turned out to be! His sister had completed the infant school (Year 2 was the highest class in the school) and was moving on to a junior school. Although the new school had been a good fit for my daughter and brought out the champion within her (with a merit award to show for it), for Ade that was not the case.

For the two years Ade spent in that school, his closest companions were the computers at school's information and communication technologies (ICT) room, where he was often sent for every conceivable and ludicrous reason. It was very distressing to see as a parent.

I believe the root problem was the fact that Ade was bigger and taller than his peers, and not challenged by the activities in the special resource unit he was placed. This was also aggravated by him being left behind when his peers moved to a new class because of limited spaces.

I guess it was easy for the school to conclude that Ade wouldn't mind this arrangement because of the autism diagnosis. After all, there is a tendency to assume that children who do not show emotions also lack empathy, just because they do not express it in a way that most people would recognise. I, however, felt Ade was not happy about having been left behind and over time I recognised that Ade indeed has a keen sense of injustice.

Ade rarely eats without his sister. Whenever I tell him he is eating a meal without his sister, the first thing he asks is, "What will my sister have?" He is not only keenly interested in the welfare of his sister but also keenly aware of others around him. If a child is crying (even if the child is a stranger), he becomes visibly distressed, and when any family member is distraught in any way, Ade notices and ask what the matter is.

We tried to partner with the school to find a way to work around the issues they had with Ade, but we made no headway. The school was not a good fit for him, and no amount of collaboration yielded any positive results. We had no choice but to contact the Special Educational Needs/Disabilities Department (SEND Department) of our Local Authority to make the necessary arrangements to have Ade transferred to a more suitable, inclusive school where he could thrive and fulfil his full potential educationally.

Consequently, to augment the school's efforts, our home became an educational centre while we waited for the SEND Department to provide us with a list of more suitable school placements.

While this back and forth with the SEND Department was still going on, we decided to move to a different borough, hoping to get him into a better school. However, the consequences of this move far outweighed the reward, as Ade ended up stranded at home for two years (from the time he was age eight till when he was age ten) with only eight hours of tuition every week!

Ensuring that Ade did not fall between the educational cracks because he was out of a school setting for that long was not easy, to say the very least. There is no denying the extent of the challenges we had to overcome and the inner strength we had to find in home-schooling him, a path we never planned to walk. So, I sucked it up and once again worked tirelessly with Ade to the best of my ability. This experience reminded me of the words of Lynn Austin: "*Smooth seas do not produce skilful sailors.*"

However, just when I was becoming very weary in my soul, as all hope of a bright future for Ade seemed to be dimming with each passing day, there came in a surprising but delightful newcomer into Ade's life.

LESSONS LEARNT: Children with autism have an unusual profile that should be recognised and accommodated by the school authority. In partial fulfilment of the conditions for obtaining a qualification in Health and Social Care, and due to my keen interest in children and autism in young people, I undertook a research project in "Co-Production in Educating Children with Autism Spectrum Disorder: Parents' Perspective". In researching for the paper, I learnt that many children with autism may:

- Have difficulty coping with the curriculum, which may be because they having trouble processing information and understanding questions and text.

- Experience sensory issues making it difficult for them to tolerate some aspects of the school environment, such as smells, noises and lighting.

- Be stressed out by a desire for perfection and see anything less than perfect as a failure.

- Find their window of tolerance reduces over time during the school day causing them to experience shut-down or melt-down.

- Find their lack of understanding of social rules can get them into trouble with teachers when they are unintentionally rude, inappropriate or give the impression they fail to respect authority.

- Take things literally, which may make them misunderstand a teacher's instructions or unable to join in with classroom jokes.

- Have a hard time decoding social cues and find sudden changes to their routine very difficult.

Unfortunately, their primary feedback is often criticism for an error they have committed, with little or no praise from others when they do things right. Learning from criticism is not the most efficient way to learn for anybody, including children with autism. This can result in behavioural problems.

These behavioural problems make it harder for children with autism to access educational and other services, and this can lead to further social isolation and frustration. This was what we experienced with Ade. Statistics from the Disabilities Trust (at the time of writing) show that 17% of all children with autism have been suspended from school, 48% of whom have been suspended three or more times, while 4% had been expelled from one or more schools (thedtgroup.org 2020).

With this high rate of exclusion, it is essential to acknowledge that the challenging behaviour displayed by some children with autism is a clear indication of the degree of stress they experience at school. Unfortunately, this is not always taken into account and, as a result, many parents experience dissatisfaction with the educational progress of autistic children.

As much as 63% of children with autism are not in the kind of school their parents believe would best support them. Parents and caregivers often struggle when faced with these situations, especially if they do not feel confident about dealing with them.

One way of resolving these issues is to ensure that parents are encouraged to become active partners and co-producers in the education of their children. Many studies have shown that close cooperation between families affected by autism and schools and other professionals can increase the parents' sense of self-efficacy and reduce their learned helplessness. This, in turn, leads to better life outcomes for children with autism and their families.

Moreover, when parents feel their voices are heard and their input is listened to, they are more motivated to engage in a productive partnership with the school. Remember, aspirational parents and good teachers are the pillars on which effective education stands!

A MEETING OF MINDS

The day started like any other day but marked the beginning of something special and made an indelible imprint in our memories. Responding to a knock on our door, I was warmly greeted by a gentle giant who introduced himself as Fred. Fred Balls was Ade's tutor, sent by the SEND Department to teach Ade while the Department continued to seek a suitable school placement. Little did we know Fred was going to give Ade wings to fly.

Fred was like a dream. I have never met a teacher so committed to educating a child with autism. Despite Ade's fierce resistance in the beginning, Fred stayed determined and focused on tutoring Ade. It appeared as if Fred had seen a vision convincing him that educating Ade was part of a higher calling.

It was indeed a battle of wills! Ade tried to push Fred away many times, as he was anxious around any stranger. However, Fred gently pulled back, knowing that it was only through resilience and empathy that Ade could progress. Fred's attitude reminded me that total commitment and courage were essential in educating a child, especially a child with autism. Fred's character also gave credence to the African adage that says: "*He that will eat the honey deep within a rock, must not consider the resultant bluntness of his axe's head.*"

For the first few weeks, Fred could not break through to Ade. I had to stick around to intervene just to try and get Ade to learn one thing or the other from Fred, who was very keen to teach. Fred believed in Ade from the start and this filled my heart with joy. Fred quickly realised Ade was mathematically gifted, even though Ade wasn't keen to work with Fred, whom he still considered an intruder.

The fact that Fred thought Ade was mathematically gifted did not come as a total surprise. A year before, at the age of seven Ade had asked me a fascinating question. On this sunny day, I had taken Ade and his sister to the park, and as we stood by the pond, watching the ducks swimming by, Ade asked me, "Mummy, what is 99 x 9?" I said I didn't know offhand, but it occurred to me that I should turn the question back to him, so I asked him for the answer.

Without hesitation, Ade said, "891." I checked the calculator on my telephone, and I saw he was correct! My jaw was on the floor and I was momentarily speechless. Once I regained my composure, I started asking him several two- and three-digits multiplication questions, which he answered without much ado, until he got bored and stopped responding.

When we got home, I told his dad. Again, Ade answered multiplication questions eagerly, until eventually he couldn't be bothered with the fuss his dad and I was making. That day marked the discovery of Ade's mathematical gifts, which he still displays whenever he is in the mood.

Anyway, back to Fred and his efforts to strike up an amicable relationship with Ade. He kept producing various ways to get Ade to feel at ease with him so that they could communicate more effectively. It seemed he was getting nowhere, until one certain day.

Fred was having one of his contemplative moments as they had yet another awkward lesson, when he noticed our piano keyboard and wondered, whether the magic of its keys might be the missing link between himself and Ade. Fred went over to the keyboard and started playing.

Oh! What a discovery! My disconnected son responded as if in a trance where his heart was opened to hear the words deep within his soul and to communicate the unsayable with his fingers. It was pure ecstasy to behold! Seeing the tutor and pupil engaged in a meeting of the minds, shattering every barrier as their fingers glided over the keys in unison as if responding to a singular beating heart! It was pure magic.

Fred burst out in laughter when this enchantment was over. This was the beginning of something beautiful, and off to the keyboard they went after each tutorial session.

> LESSONS LEARNT: Skills are often uneven in autism. A child with autism may be good at one thing and poor at another, and abilities in such children vary greatly. This was what we saw with Ade. A child with autism can easily be viewed as a bundle of deficits, paying little attention to their sometimes obvious but often easy-to-miss talents. However, it is imperative to look beyond the child's weaknesses and take time to recognise and develop the child's talents, just as Fred was able to notice and start to nurture Ade's musical and mathematical giftedness. Developing talents and improving skills in a child with autism is advantageous to everyone.

If a child becomes fixated on a thing, then use that fixation to motivate learning other skills. One needs to help a child to discover the gifts and talents within them and to sharpen and expand them until the child is empowered to use their own gifts to the best of their ability. It took Fred's grit and compassion to break down the barriers between him and Ade before he could draw out the talents and gifts locked deep within Ade's mind.

Who would have thought Fred's approach of using the piano as a means to connect with Ade would lead to an inspiring friendship between them, igniting Ade's desire to learn and, ultimately, the development of many skills within Ade? Music proved to be the perfect medium for shedding light on who Ade was from inside out and at the same time has infused Ade's life with something he truly cherishes!

For a while, I thought about how playing music on a keyboard, a single instrument producing abstract patterns in sound, could foster such a deep bond between Fred and Ade. How could it promote self-awareness in Ade, help him develop emotional literacy and facilitate social interaction? I realised it was because music is a language beyond words, whose sequences of notes are free to convey pure emotion, unfettered by the need for semantic understanding.

For Fred, who had open ears and willingness to engage with children with autism, I believe music offered a means of breaking down barriers to embrace Ade's different ways of thinking, thereby unearthing a talented and soulful pianist. I will always be truly grateful for that!

UNWANTED BUT NOT UNPLEASANT

Newtons law of motion states that every object in a state of uniform motion will remain in that state of motion unless an external force act on it. Why did an external force have to disturb the fine dance between Fred and Ade? Just when Fred and Ade finally found a rhythm to their relationship, the SEND Department decided it was time for a change.

"Oh God have mercy," I muttered as I wept over the decision. "This is simply wrong," I said to his dad. I wrote letters in protest to the SEND Department. No matter how passionately I pleaded and however well-reasoned and evidential I thought my letters were, the SEND Department still replaced Fred with Jennifer, Kate and Janet (not their real names).

While Kate and Janet were kind staff that ticked boxes, Jennifer was different. She brought with her kindness and warmth. She was never impatient with Ade, she worked at his pace and when she saw he was ready, she introduced him to Mathletics and Reading Eggs (both computer-based educational programmes). These programmes expanded Ade's learning and academic exposure. Jennifer also taught him good morals and encouraged his love for music.

Ade warmed to Jennifer, he was drawn to her calm and gentle approach. But thank God for Fred, who embodied the three qualities Warren Buffett said he looks for in the people he wants to hire: integrity, intelligence and energy. For Fred, true to his promise, continued to come every Saturday to teach Ade the piano.

So, the women taught him academic subjects during the week and Fred taught him music on Saturdays. What a fine balance this turned out to be, for what I first thought was a setback (replacing Fred with the women) ended up taking Ade to greater heights. This arrangement continued for two years.

> LESSONS LEARNT: Change can be good for your child. Psychologist William James once said that most people live in a restricted circle of their full potential. That could have easily been Ade's story, orchestrated by my strong desire for stability and continuity for him. I did not want any tutor apart from Fred to get involved with Ade's education, as I was attuned to the delicate dance between Fred and Ade.

I tried all I could to push against the unexpected change introduced by the SEND Department, as I felt it would be a force of destruction. Instead, it opened Ade up to a world of pleasant possibilities, broadened his horizons educationally and allowed him to have social interactions with more people.

So I wonder in how many ways we prevent our children with autism from experiencing the full breadth of their capabilities or maximising their full potential because we allow fear and rigidity to keep them living within the box of familiarity, rather than being brave enough to allow them into a world of wider possibilities, just as happened for Ade.

UNACCEPTABLE!

We remained committed to collaborating with the SEND Department for a school placement for Ade. However, this was a strain because the SEND Department appeared to be against getting Ade settled in a suitable school. It was an agonising period. It was very difficult getting the necessary cooperation from the SEND Department and there was little support for struggling parents. I found this particularly irritating because, while my job at that time involved supporting and advocating for children and young children in the special educational needs system in a local authority, I found myself without any support for Ade in our own local authority.

It was not that there was no available support, but it was that it was spread so thin that it was very little use to me. It was further frustrating in that, although I had access to information and manpower in the borough where I worked, it wasn't on all fours with the system of the borough where we lived.

What an irony. Here was I, collaborating with the local authority and other professionals on behalf of other people's children and young people to ensure they had better educational outcomes, yet my son was left without a school from age eight to age ten. Even though our local authority had an Information, Advice and Support Service (IASS) that offered a service similar to the one I was delivering, it was very difficult to access their service. For one, the advocates in the IASS were too few compared to the size of the borough. Consequently, they were often not available, and their service was likely to be a one-off, as opposed to going all the way to help you achieve your desired outcome (in this case getting Ade into a school). One wondered why someone would even bother contacting them.

Having seen I wasn't going to get much support from the local SEND Department, I started doing research and sending emails. The level of communication from the SEND Department left a lot to be desired. Often, my emails were ignored, and when they were finally replied to, there were no apologies for failing to even acknowledge their receipt. It was an incredibly stressful time, but I refused to give up. My training as a solicitor was particularly useful, as I was able to send the SEND Department very detailed documents quoting relevant laws about the local authority's responsibility to educate a child with special educational needs and the need to work with us, Ade's parents, as joint stakeholders.

It was an exhausting and uphill battle trying to get the SEND Department to produce a list of suitable schools, but the persistence paid off. They finally provided us with a list of three schools that the

Department considered suitable for Ade. Unfortunately, none of the schools were suitable on our inspection. For example, when we met him, the head of one of the schools told us our son did not fit the criteria for the school, and that he was going to send a letter to the SEND Department to that effect.

I refused to the deterred by the non-committal attitude of the SEND department and renewed my determination to ensure that Ade got into a school where he would have a fighting chance to succeed, thrive and develop skills needed for an independent life. And so, we persevered.

In this back and forth, the SEND department let us apply to a school that went up to A-level, so Ade could attend the school from Year 5 (where he was then) to the age of 18. Our hearts were flooded with joy with the thought of this fantastic opportunity! You can only imagine how deflated we felt when we found out the so-called opportunity was a hoax.

We visited the school, only to get a visit from the school's representatives informing us that the school felt they could not meet Ade's needs. I went berserk because the school was known to cater to children with autism, ranging from those who were high functioning to those who were severely impacted. I had visited the school and knew for sure that Ade did not fall below the level of the children supported by the school, so for the SEND Department to then turn around to say the school could not meet Ade's needs was ludicrous.

It felt like they had pulled the carpet from under our feet. We had been denied an educational setting for Ade for two years and there is just so much one can take. We decided it was time to escalate matters to the Member of Parliament (MP) for our area .

LESSONS LEARNT: An Statement of Educational Needs (Statement) (all children on Statement have now been transferred to Education, Health and Care Plan (EHC Plan)) is pivotal in securing the right educational environment for a child with autism. The way Ade's Statement was worded after his experience at his earlier school hindered him from accessing a good school for two years! I say this because, the kind of schools the Department sent us to visit and consider for Ade were schools for children with social, emotional and mental health needs which were clearly not right for him as attested to by one of the schools' principal. Yet as his Statement profiled him as a child with unmanageable emotions and serious behavioural issue, most suitable school won't even cast an eye over him. Hence, the SEND Department's kept sending us on a wild-goose chase looking for a school placement for two whole year until his Statement was transferred to an EHC Plan.

While getting a child diagnosed and having their needs detailed in their EHC Plan can enable the child to access the right educational support, as well as facilitate an understanding of their behavioural traits and how to address with them, the diagnosis, as well as their EHC Plan, must never be presented in a way that prevents access to a suitable school placement, as happened with Ade. The only way Ade was able to overcome this hurdle and access a suitable school was to ensure that when his Statement was transferred to an EHC Plan it gave a holistic picture of him. But how?

Fortunately, whilst researching, I came across a Regulation that obliged Local Authority transferring a child or young person from a Statement to an EHC Plan to conduct a "Transfer Review". To achieve this a Local Authority must carry out a EHC needs assessment which simply means that they have to seek information and advice from the child's parents, professionals working with the child, their school (in Ade's case his tutors) to determine: the child's needs, the provisions vital to meet the needs and the outcomes expected to be achieved by the child (Transition to the new 0 to 25 special educational needs and disability system. Departmental advice for local authorities and their partner. 3rd Edition (2014). The SEND Department of our Local Authority accepted my findings, and commissioned the Speech and Language Therapist, the Educational Psychologist, the Paediatrician and his tutors to observe him and write report of their findings.

Based on these reports together with our (his parents) submission about Ade, EHC Plan was written down to the last detail of his learning needs, his challenges as well as his strengths. Without that, I do not think he would have been able to access the exceptional support that held the key to the new opportunities he was able to access later.

This encapsulates in my mind the thought that parents need to advocate for their children and must be willing to go the extra mile to ensure good education and life outcomes.

I have come to discover that as a parent, each child is different. I also learnt the importance of seeking help where necessary to ensure that Ade could access the necessary support and attain the best educational and life outcomes. Who knows what the outcome would have been for Ade if we had not managed to get his EHC Plan rewritten, considering the earlier schools that the SEND department was suggesting to us? Unimaginable!

THIS IS IT!

When our MP got our letter explaining the situation Ade was in, he was appalled that Ade had been out of school for that long without an end in view. He wrote back to us saying how sorry he was to hear about our case and he also escalated the matter to the Secretary of State for Education. Both him and the Secretary of State for Education got in touched the SEND department requiring answers to why Ade has been out of school placement for so long . To cut to the chase, the SEND department under a new manager arranged a meeting with us and out of what appeared like thin air, a list of suitable schools was produced.

We were delighted that finally there appeared to be light at the end of the tunnel! We sprang into action and visited the schools suggested. The moment we went in, I knew we had finally found the one. "This is it!" I said excitedly as we were taken round Valley Invicta school. Hope rose within me, I felt certain that this school had wonderful things in store for Ade. Interestingly, that was exactly how his dad felt too.

Yes! It turned out just as we thought, and it reminded me of the poem I had written while we were still awaiting a school placement for Ade. This poem (or should I say this declaration) entitled "*Yes, He Will*" declared that Ade would reach great heights irrespective of autism and the many challenges he was facing.

Within a few days of inspecting the school, Ade was admitted, and he started to attend. As soon as Ade settled into school (this was the 2nd term of Year 5), we were resolute that he was going to sit the Year 6 SAT (Statutory Assessment Test). We refused to let the fact that he had been at home for the last two years (and barely accessed the national curriculum in his last year in school) to deter us from expecting Ade to sit his Year 6 SAT, with the right support.

Believe me, it was an uphill task, but we knew that with God and hard work, the dream of Ade sitting and passing his SAT exams could be a reality. As Christopher Reeves once said: "*So many of our dreams at first seem impossible, then they seem improbable and then when we summon the will, they soon become inevitable.*" Little did I know what fate had in store.

LESSONS LEARNT: One of the hardest things for a parent with a child with autism is finding the right school. A child needs an educational environment where their talents will be developed, where the love for learning will be ignited and, most importantly, where the child will be well nurtured. This can only be achieved where the school has a good understanding of the child's uniqueness and qualities.

Valley Invicta School ticked all these boxes and much more. Not only did the school have an amazing understanding of Ade's uniqueness, but they were also willing to tailor both the curriculum and the disciplinary process to his needs. When a child displays challenging behaviour, the child is communicating that he has a problem, not that he is a problem. No child should be punished for their needs. Valley Invicta understood this principle and for that I am eternally grateful.

Sending Ade to Valley Invicta in the morning no longer equated to being on edge, wondering if I was going to get a call saying there was a problem. This time, I was free to breathe and free to be. I look forward to a time where all parents with a child with autism can say unequivocally that this is their experience.

Valley Invicta will always be remembered by us as a place where Ade metamorphosed from a caterpillar to a butterfly, and where he began relating to the wider world!

CHARTING THE COURSE

Often, things we think we need to travel to find instead come to find us. This was the situation I found myself in. Barely six months after Ade started school, and a month into his Year 6, while I was still considering how best to support Ade, I started working in schools.

This was a real change in my career, which I had put on hold (as a qualified solicitor with a Master's degree in law and a Diploma in Health and Social Care), but it turned out to be an immense help to Ade's academic progression as I was able to access the right information about effective ways to prepare Ade for his SAT. I bought all the recommended books and worked assiduously with Ade. Sometimes, preparing him was extremely daunting but I found succour in the words of Colin Powell: *"a dream does not become reality through magic. It takes determination, and hard work."*

I had to learn to think things through with Ade and to praise him whenever I saw him struggling or finding the work challenging. His autism means Ade finds some things difficult, including reading comprehension. Keeping the dream alive helped us to weather these difficulties.

I learnt that to help Ade discover and nurture his strengths and abilities, I needed to pay enough attention to him so I could acknowledge and focus on his unique learning style. In this voyage, I discovered that Ade was a visual learner, that is, in addition to written text, he liked to be shown what he is been taught. Therefore, we used a lot of DVDs and online videos in tutoring him. It is amazing how much knowledge he gained using this method.

One day, while studying, I read about someone talking about Calendrical savants. Calendrical savants are people who can name the weekdays for dates from different years with remarkable speed, accuracy and without the need to check a calendar. The article then said that these savants have often been also diagnosed with autism.

Could this also be true with Ade? We had experienced his mathematical prowess and his musical gifts, but could he also be a calendrical savant? In my curiosity, whilst teaching Ade some mathematical concepts, I casually asked Ade what day of the week a particular date fell on and to my utter amazement, he told me the day the given date it was! I was completely flabbergasted! I was left speechless for a while. It was such a surreal moment, but Ade was unaware that he had done something almost magical. I asked him a couple more and each time without any hesitation, he told me what day of the week each date fell on while I, in a state of total disbelief, checked my phone. Every single answer he gave was correct.

I was so shocked by the pure display of genius by Ade, and impressed with the effortless brilliance, that I just carried on with our maths lesson, but my heart couldn't stop wondering about this amazing discovery. Oh, how my heart was yelling to share this discovery with his dad, who was out when the whole drama was going on. When he got home, he saw my face was beaming with excitement and could not but wonder what was going on. Grinning from ear and ear, I told him what had happened, and he could scarcely believe it. He was simply blown away by this discovery. Cheetah-swift, his dad dashed to where Ade was, and he kept asking Ade the day for different dates and Ade gave the answers without blinking an eyelid. Even today, he can still tell you in a twinkle of an eye.

It is also interesting that although Ade can appear to be restless to outsiders due to his constant movement, at home, he is so organised. Every evening, he hangs his uniform and brings out his undergarments, so he does not have to look for anything in the morning. When we are travelling as a family, he is the organiser. He makes sure we pack all that is needed for the trip and when we are coming back home, he ensures that we do not leave any of our stuff behind.

This brings to mind an experience when Ade was five years old. I had gone to pick Ade from school when his teacher called me aside and said she felt Ade had a squint in one of his eyes and, from her experience, he might need a pair of glasses to correct it. A river of worry came rushing through my mind. I can't say what was the major cause of the worry. Was it the fact that Ade had a squint and might require glasses? Or was it that I did not know how I was going to get a child diagnosed with autism to manage the use of his prescription glasses without breaking them, losing them or, worse still, hurting himself?

My fear that he might need a pair of glasses was confirmed by the ophthalmologist. The ophthalmologist that examined Ade gave him a strong prescription, which meant Ade was given very thick lenses straight away, and the ophthalmologist even wondered how Ade had managed without glasses for that long.

Thankfully, my second fear never materialised. To my greatest amazement and relief, he has not only been able to keep his glasses safe from breaking but to able to keep from losing them. In fact, in the over seven years he has been wearing glasses we have only had to go looking for the glasses only a couple of times. Ade's abilities to organise his things continue to dazzle me in many ways.

In my reflective moments, I am always awestruck by Ade's giftedness and the way he overcomes the daily challenges he faces.

There is always some predicament when raising a neurodiverse child! This brings to mind the insightful words of Daniel Defoe: *"Invest in the human soul. Who knows, it might be a diamond in the rough."* This is further corroborated by the wise words of Thomas Browne: *"Rough diamonds may sometimes be mistaken for worthless pebbles."*

The wisdom of these words provided me with the strength to carry on. The months rolled by. Despite the challenges and uncertainties in getting him ready for the SAT we stayed the course. We forged ahead, holding on to the belief that one day, soon, the dream of seeing Ade sitting and passing his SAT would be a reality, no matter how challenging and emotionally tasking the preparation might be.

LESSONS LEARNT. Living with a child with autism is a conundrum, as joyful moments are interwoven with moments of utter despair. Parents find themselves oscillating between awareness of their child's dysfunction and recognising his or her advanced skills. How is it possible for extraordinary ability and giftedness to co-exist in jarring juxtaposition with incapacitating social and learning disability in the same individual? The answer is not simple!

Thankfully, a diagnosis of autism does not take away giftedness! Of all the features of autism, none is more widely admired than the remarkable talents often displayed by an individual with autism. In popular accounts of autism, the existence of extraordinary talent in art, music, mathematics calendar calculation or memory are reported (often referred to as savant skills). Indeed, we need to think beyond the diagnosis and instead investigate the abilities of a child, rather than focusing on the disabling limitations and then being shocked when the child displays abilities!

This philosophy, though empowering, does not immunise one from the unique set of challenges one experiences in raising a child with autism. I quickly realised that if I were to be an effective primary educator, I had to develop a set of skills that would help me teach Ade life skills and draw out the best in him. I researched constantly, I asked for help, I listened to advice and I even obtained a certification in Applied Behaviour Analysis.

I started noticing the same set of recommendations, often referred to as core strategies, for promoting and supporting the emotional, intellectual, social, and cognitive development of children, including those with autism. These core strategies are preparing for success, rewards and consequences, reflective listening, and descriptive praise.

Descriptive praise is considered to be the most powerful motivator. It is telling your child exactly what you are complimenting them for. For example, instead of just saying "Well done!" you say, "Well done for persevering with your work, even though you found it a bit hard." That way, the child understands precisely why you are praising them, and it sounds more genuine than when you give them non-specific praise. The catch here is that you have to be observant to notice every effort they make at doing the right thing. It sounds challenging to do but I can testify that it works in motivating children, especially one with autism, to cooperate and do their best. This is because children are more likely to repeat the behaviour that was praised, and so they strive to make such behaviour part of their identity.

Words are extremely powerful in raising a person's self-worth, and this is true even for non-neurotypical individuals with autism. One could almost think of descriptive praise as affirmative brainwashing, because by articulating your child's strengths and gifts when you descriptively praise her, you and your child begin to believe it.

I was so intrigued by these strategies that I decided to put them to use, using the descriptive praise as a particular anchor as Ade prepared for his SAT and music exams. The dividends we reaped were so impressive that we are still practising them to this day.

I now feel so empowered by these strategies that I have extended myself to start preparing Ade for adulthood. I have started to teach him life skills such as being organised, making independent decisions and making simple meals. With time we and the professionals involved with Ade will have done enough to help him achieve the best possible outcomes in employment, independent living, health and community participation.

WHAT A GREAT COACH INDEED!

"A good coach can change a game; a great coach can change a life."
John Wooden

Let's pause here and thank Fred, the great coach. Fred is indeed a great coach, for he saw a great pianist in Ade, and he continues to play a huge part in making him just that! For weekends in, weekends out, Fred came to teach Ade the piano. Even when abroad, he called and emailed to ensure that Ade was still taking piano lessons and consistently practising on his keyboard.

"Let's enter him for Grade 1 piano exams," Fred suggested when he got back from his travels.

"Fred, you know his piano ability best, and we trust your judgement," I replied apprehensively. I was apprehensive, not because I didn't trust Fred, but because having a child diagnosed with autism means you worry about how your child will cope with things that are simple for "neurotypical" children. Things like how he would stay focused on the piano pieces, learn them before the exams, whether he would even want to learn the notes and how he would handle the exam situation itself! Oh! How I longed for Ade to give full expression to his musical ability!

Despite my apprehension, we entered him for the Grade 1 piano exams because I believed that Fred knew Ade well enough to say whether Ade was ready to take the piano exams. For my part, I encouraged Ade to practice his chosen pieces for the exams, and those were what we listened to in the car whilst commuting.

So, as Ade prepared for his Year 6 SAT, he was also preparing for his piano exams and both exams were just a month apart. Talk about pressure!

"Ade has a perfect pitch!" Fred continued to declare with delight, although I had little idea what that meant. I was simply happy that Ade was enjoying playing and practising his keyboard consistently without fuss, while we continued to practise with past question papers for his Year 6 SAT. So, through the uncertainties and apprehensions, we kept moving forward.

I am so grateful to fate for bringing Fred across Ade's path. There is this meeting of minds between them that is so beautiful to watch. Fred has been a great coach to Ade and he constantly encourages him to aim for the stars. Because Fred believed in Ade, Ade started to fly! What a difference the presence of Fred has made in Ade's life! Fred believed, then Ade believed, and together they triggered Ade's love for piano and, most importantly, created a friendship that has stood the test of time.

LESSONS LEARNT: Having a caring coach or teacher to whom a child with autism feels connected and who is committed to helping the child mature and maximise his potential is a treasure of unqualifiable value. I have learnt that for children with autism to gain much ground, they need to have in their life wise men and women who understand their uniqueness, and who are dedicated enough to help them see their own abilities and talents.

Fred freely gave of his time to Ade no matter how busy his schedule was. No obstacle was ever too great for Fred to overcome to fulfil his promise to give Ade music lessons. Oceans could not stop him, and the challenges of autism seemed like child's play compared to his determination to make a pianist of Ade.

Through patience and encouragement, Fred ignited Ade's passion for learning and music and he constantly derived ways to keep Ade motivated.

However, the best gift Fred gave Ade was the gift of total, unconditional and true friendship, which keeps getting better like a wine that becomes more valuable with age.

So, for us, our strong wise man is the gentle giant Fred and I believe that having Fred in Ade's life have played a major role in his progress and success so far.

SUPPORT CAN COME FROM UNUSUAL PLACES

Who would have thought Ade's sister Ademurewa, who was just fourteen and a half months older than him, would turn out to be such a great help in raising Ade? Her love for Ade never ceases to amaze me. She was always looking out for Ade, right from when she was very young. I remember when she was four years old and Ade was three, we were out all day and when we got home, I could not easily find Ade's pyjama bottom. I gave him his pyjama top and one of his regular trousers but Ademurewa was having none of it. She told me Ade had not been properly dressed for bed and I could not put him to sleep without it. She was so emphatic about the need for Ade to be properly dressed that the tiredness flew out of the window as I set about finding his pyjama bottom, and I did.

Whenever we are on the go, Ademurewa always keeps an eye out for Ade, especially when he was younger and was keen on going on adventures. You would hear Ademurewa say, "stay here, where Mummy can see you." If I have to take my eyes off him for a minute,

I know she will keep watch over him. When they are eating and my daughter gets something for herself, she will also get another for Ade.

It is also interesting to see how much influence she has on Ade. I remember being very concerned about his handwriting, even until he was about nine years old because it was nothing short of a chicken scratch. When I mentioned it to his teacher, she said it was an autism spectrum issue and nothing to worry about. I was not impressed with the teacher's fixed mindset towards Ade's handwriting, so I knew I was not going to get much support from her.

Fortunately, I have a sister who runs a school abroad and I asked her to send me handwriting materials to support my effort to get Ade to write more legibly. Thinking we were going to have to work on his handwriting for a long time to get up to scratch. I made it a duty to get him to practice daily. To my surprise, however, Ade started writing in beautiful cursive within a short time.

I knew it wasn't the few practice sessions that had led to this transformation, rather it was something more subtle but more powerful. He wanted to write like his sister! Ademurewa's handwriting had always been commended as beautiful by her teachers from a very young age. Ade's desire to write like her got him writing legibly! I couldn't have done it better. What an influence!

Realising that Ademurewa was one of the greatest role models in Ade's life, I knew that if I could get her to model the desired behaviour, he would, in time, follow suit. Whatever Ademurewa is doing, Ade will also try to do, and this has resulted in learning many life skills and enjoying spending quality time with his precious sister.

I have often teased Ademurewa for acting as Ade's policewoman, as she will let me know if he was doing what he was not supposed to do when I was not there. So much so that Ade knew he couldn't get away with doing something in front of his sister without Ademurewa pointing it out and letting me know about it. This has kept him on the straight and narrow in many ways!

Ademurewa also accommodates and respects Ade's preferences and differences. For example, if she has asked to eat something that she knows her brother does not like to eat, her next question will be, "but what will Ade eat?" If she is eating vegetables that Ade does not like, she will encourage him to eat them, telling him they are good for him. She has successfully got him to eat more vegetables than anyone in this way.

I am impressed by how they fit into each other's daily routines. When it is time for homework and Ade would rather do something else, Ademurewa gets on with her work and then encourages Ade to do the same, thereby reducing the effort I have to make to get him to work.

They are best friends and rarely disagree. I am amazed by how much interest Ademurewa takes in Ade's passions, and vice versa. They are willing to try what makes the other one happy. The most important thing for them is to be together, whatever the activity.

I am extremely grateful for the subtle but powerful influence of my precious princess Ademurewa on Ade. The support I have had from her in raising Ade has been amazing and none of which I take for granted. I love you to the moon and back my darling daughter, you have been a great pillar of support in ensuring that Ade reaches for the stars!

> LESSONS LEARNT: When a child is diagnosed with autism, everyone in the family is affected. Family resources must not only be directed at the autistic child but also to ensure as full and as rich a life as possible for all family members. This is because the entire family's involvement is one of the most critical and essential elements in improving outcomes for a child with autism. Siblings are the most significant members of the family, second only to the parents, and the sibling relationship is unique in many ways.

Siblings are a very important part of child development, as the children share in each other's everyday experiences as companions, confidantes, combatants and role models. They are available to express feelings and support and offer friendship. For those of us who have brothers and sisters, that relationship is often the longest we will have in our life, especially as often we are close in age and we age and grow together.

In the different roles we assume as siblings, we often have direct effects on one another's development, as social partners, role models, judges of acceptable or unacceptable behaviours, and guides to the social world outside the reaches of our family's influence. We also influence one another indirectly through our impact on the larger family dynamics, where we may serve as building blocks of the family structure, influence the social climate of the family, hold a favoured family niche, contribute to family resources or provide training in a variety of behaviours. All these give us copious opportunities to shape one another's behaviour and socio-emotional development and adjustment.

Considering the many positive impacts siblings have on each other, I have always encouraged my children to develop strategies to relate to each other, and to help themselves and the functioning of the family as a whole. For example, I encourage them to play games they both enjoy and to follow similar routines. This has been fundamental in developing their play skills, positive interactions, social behaviour and shared interests, thereby helping them forge a sense of togetherness. Together they are stronger, and that makes for an excellent life-long support team.

SITTING THE EXAMS

"Can Ade come early to school next week? All pupils are encouraged to come early to have some quiet time before starting their SAT," his teacher enquired.

"Sure, we'll arrange to bring him early," I replied thinking: "Wow, the SAT is finally here!"

Sure enough, the SAT week came, we woke early and prayed for Ade. Ade stayed cheerful and bright throughout the exams week and did not complain when we did a bit of revision the day before each paper. O Lord, how great Thou art, I prayed, that Ade diagnosed with autism who did not talk nor understand until he was five years, who was out of school for two years and seemed to have major trouble settling down, is now sitting his SAT!

Every day, when Ade came back from his SAT exams, I was eager to know how his exams had gone and his usual reply was: "It was fine." This went on until the end of the week. The weekend finally came, and the family got some rest. Ade was looking forward to the following week when he and his classmates were scheduled to take part in many fun post-exam activities.

While still basking in the euphoria of the fun he had had at school, Ade had to continue to practise for his piano exams. "Please get Ade to the exams centre at least 15 minutes before the exams," Fred pleaded. Based on this recommendation, I decided to get Ade to the centre at least 30 minutes before.

As we entered the waiting room, Ade went straight to the piano and as soon as he touched the piano, his fingers seemed to caress the keys, producing mesmerising sounds. For the first time, I appreciated Fred's excitement, as I came to understand what he meant when he said that Ade had a perfect pitch. I sat enthralled by what Ade could produce on the grand piano (as he had been using the keyboard to practise at home).

"Wow! That was amazing!" I told Ade. Even before Ade went in for his exams, I knew I had a talented pianist for a son, and I believed the examiner would hear that too. After the examination, I took him home confident that later news about the exams would be goods.

LESSONS LEARNT: Rewards bring rewards. As I said earlier, there are some core strategies for promoting and supporting the emotional, intellectual, social and emotional development of a child with or without autism. Parents may hope that force, confrontation, name-calling, negative phrasing, shouting, threatening or warning children will motivate them, but they do not. Threats can boomerang because children (like Ade) with autism often do not have the built-in desire to please others. They often do not understand why they should do something they do not want to do just because it is asked of them.

They may also feel anxious when asked to do something unfamiliar and prefer to do activities they know and enjoy because it feels safe. In any case, we do not want our children to do the right thing merely out of fear of the consequences. So, we are left wondering how we can motivate a child with autism to overcome their resistance to learning new skills or to become more cooperative.

Rewarding good behaviour seems to offer some answers. A reward or positive reinforcement is an incentive given to a child who follows some request for behavioural change. The aim is to increase the chances of the child responding to the changed behaviour. Rewards then form an important part of teaching a child with autism various life skills, because nearly all children will respond to meaningful rewards, and Ade was no exception.

Thus, rewards accompanied by praise should be given once the desired behaviour has occurred. This is likely to shape the child's future behaviour and make the child aware of the specific reason why they were rewarded. Such a reward might be something to play with, something to look at, something to smell, something to do or something to eat (although food rewards should be used sparingly).

For example, when I was preparing Ade for his SAT, I would tell him at the start of the session that if he completed the set task, he could have time on the computer to create any presentation he liked. Immediately when he completed his task, I would praise him for completing his task and tell him he could use the computer as promised. This strategy worked very well throughout and was instrumental in getting through the syllabus with Ade before he sat his exams.

However, using rewards should not become an obstacle that stops children from exploring and evoking their natural motivations and confidence because they have learnt from experience that behaving according to our dictates earns rewards. The key is to plan for the process of generalising a learnt behaviour and to fade rewards out over time.

One of the ways to solve this problem is to accept our children, quirks and all. Rather than focusing on how a child with autism is different from other children, what they may be "missing" and how you can fix them, you need to practice acceptance. For me, I noticed Ade was curious and wanted to know why he had to do what he was being asked to do. I have learnt to explain the reasons behind my requests. Rather than getting upset, I am happy as long as Ade does the work after the explanation. Feeling unconditionally loved and accepted will help your child more than anything else you can do for them.

This is so important because acceptance affects a child's self-esteem, as it is difficult for children to flourish and learn when they are always made to feel like they are broken and in need of being fixed. This mindset becomes a barrier to success, preventing them from trying new things if they are sure that all they will hear is how they got it wrong, no matter how nicely we think we phrase that message.

It is because children with autism are made to feel broken by society that so many of them end up developing depression and mental health issues. I always say that it is the societal conditioning, not the autism itself, that individuals with autism find most damaging. To bring out the best in our children, we must be willing to see their strengths and acknowledge that there is more than one right way to do most things.

HE DID IT!

We awaited the news of his piano exams, not with anxiety but with excitement, as we knew that his piano result would be out before his SAT result. Then the wait was over! Ten days after the day of his piano exams, we received the good news that Ade had indeed passed his piano exams! What a sweet experience to have your conviction confirmed! We were overjoyed. We shared this news with his school and continued to await his SAT result.

The school had many activities planned for the end of the term, sports day, the Year 6 The Lion King production and the school leavers' assembly. The sports day left me crushed. Ade's Learning Support Assistant held on to Ade's hands and she supported him to do all the sporting activities. She held his hands in running the races, in throwing the javelin and in jumping during the long jump making him look like the school clown. This was even more painful to watch because of his very tall frame, which made him stick out like a sore thumb. This lit a fire in my belly, and I was fuming, but I decided to keep my peace and process my thoughts.

That evening, I collected myself and in a non-sentimental but professional way, I wrote a letter to his class teacher expressing my displeasure and stating categorically that if he could not be encouraged to participate in the Year 6 Lion King production independently, then she should let me know so that I could keep him at home and not allow him to be subjected to another ridicule.

I am pleased to say that my letter seemed to have made a difference. Ade came out to read lines from the production and to take part in the choreography. Yes, he missed some steps, but who cares! Ade was achieving another milestone right before us. Who would have thought Ade would take part in a school production a few years ago? Then I thought, Tony Evans was very insightful when he said, "*you need to understand that life is not what you're given, it's what you create, what you overcome and what you achieve that makes it beautiful.*"

While I was still rejoicing in his production performance, Ade's SAT result finally came out. Boom! What a way to end his Valley Invicta School career. A school to whom we prayerfully released Ade, a school we were optimistic about, a school we believed held remarkable things in store for him and, oh boy, we were not disappointed!

As we opened his SAT results envelope, the letters and figures that greeted us made us erupt in laughter of joy and hope. Hope that indeed there was greatness in everyone, hope that setbacks were not forever, hope that high expectations and aspirations for Ade was not living in denial, hope that my declarations in my poem for Ade were not a mirage, hope that by and by more and more of my declarations about Ade in that poem would come about. As Earl Nightingale said, *"Never give up on a dream just because of the time it will take to accomplish it."*

As I call to mind the pronouncement of the paediatrician, "Your son has autism," and remember how hopeless and helpless I felt those many years ago, I am amazed by how far Ade has come, despite the autism and its accompanying challenges.

I reflect on all these years and all that we and Ade have gone through and how far we have come, I have come to appreciate the wisdom in Dr Temple Grandin's word: *"Your child with autism has unlimited potential, just like everyone else."*

Although there is still a long distance to travel, I choose to move forward, working with hope and believing that He who has begun these good works will be faithful to Ade even as Ade moves on to secondary school!

EPILOGUE

Afterwards, I realised that Ade passing his SAT and music exams had a lot to do with my thoughts and expectations. I believed he could, I gave my best to ensure that he could, and he did! What made the greatest impact on Ade's growth, thriving and being a happy person was not any intervention, treatment, diet or therapy (as important as these are), but was all about my perception of him. If we cannot see our child with autism as an interesting, inherently capable and valuable member of the family then no amount of education or therapy we expose them to will matter.

As challenging as raising a child with autism can be, one should never give up. Do not jump to conclusions about what life is going to be like for your child. Like everyone else, a child with autism has an entire lifetime to grow and develop their abilities. With Ade, there was no assurance that he would regain reflective and expressive language, but apparently out of the blue he developed functional language. Appreciate and highlight what the child can do rather than what they cannot do.

That said, it cannot be overemphasised that caring for a child with autism demands mental, emotional and physical energy, as well as a lot of time, which may lead to feeling overwhelmed, fatigued, discouraged or stressed out. These can impair executive function, reduce patience and induce forgetfulness thereby impeding one's ability to cope with life's daily demands. So, it is essential to take care of oneself. Doing all one can to stay emotionally, mentally and physically strong for as long as possible is crucial to being the best parent for a child with autism.

Take care of yourself too. Strategies for managing the demands of caring for a child with autism include:

- Making out time to catch up on some of that lost sleep.

- Doing something fun daily.

- Taking time to pray.

- Investing in a hobby (reading, journaling, gardening and so on).

- Doing some form of exercise.

- Visiting happy places either physically or mentally.

- Practising gratefulness.

- Maintaining a sense of humour.

- Asking for help when needed.

- Going for counselling (depending on your needs).

- Having regular medical check-up.

Do not neglect your health, which tends to be put on the backburner when you have a child with autism. Remember the advice given in the aeroplane is that if there is an emergency, you put on your oxygen mask before putting on your child.

Most important of all, believe in your child so they can develop the self-belief needed to hold on to their dreams, which shape each person's future. Many children with autism have unique talents and strengths such as:

- Hyperlexia (that is the ability to read at a very young age).

- The ability to learn and think visually.

- The ability to learn and memorise a large amount of information quickly and retain it for a long time.

- The ability to excel in logical and technical subjects like science and mathematics.

- The ability to pay attention to details and be precise.

- Exceptional problem-solving, reliability and honesty.

Some of these strengths and abilities are hidden under the layers of their disabilities (weaknesses), whilst others are so obvious that they are easy to miss because of the mindset that helping children with autism overcome their weaknesses must be the priority.

Beyond addressing Ade's intellectual learning style, I realised it is also important to understand the other characteristics that affect the way Ade thinks, his behaviour and motivation. These include addressing issues such as what makes sense to Ade, what he cares about and his perspectives about the world around him.

I cannot say I fully understand what makes Ade tick, but I have come to view him as a rose unfolding its petals as he continues to blossom and mature. So, as Ade leaves primary school and moves on to secondary school, marking the end of one chapter and beginning of another, who knows what adventure awaits us?

REFERENCES AND ADDITIONAL RESOURCES

1. A spectrum of Spectrum of Harmful Interventions for Autism: A Short Report (Updated March 2018) available at https://westminsterautismcommission.files.wordpress.com/2018/03/a-spectrum-of-harmful-interventions-web-version.pdf

2. Advice about school: Choosing a school for your child (Page last reviewed: 18 April 2019) Available at https://www.nhs.uk/conditions/autism/autism-and-everyday-life/school/

3. Adams, J. B, PhD, Edelson, S. M. Ph.D., Grandin, T. Ph.D., Rimland, & B. Ph.D., Johnson, J. Advice for Parents: Evidence-based Treatment During Early Intervention 7 Feb 2020 Autism Research Institute– Available at https://www.autism.org/advice-for-parents/

4. Amaral, D.G . (2017), Examining the Causes of Autism. Available at: https://www.ncbi.nlm.nih.gov/pmc/articles/PMC5501015/

5. Arky, B. (2018) Autism Plus Wandering published by the Child Mind Institute (an institute based in the United States of America. Available at: https://childmind.org/article/autism-plus-wandering/ (Accessed on 25th September 2020).

6. Autism: The management and support of children of children and young people on autism spectrum (2013). NICE Clinical Guideline 170. Available at: https://www.nice.org.uk/guidance/CG170 (Accessed on 25th September 2020)

7. Baxter, R. Hughes, L. International Journal of Clinical Pediatrics, ISSN 1927-1255 print, 1927-1263 online Open Access, Article copyright, the authors, Journal compilation copyright. Int J Clin Pediatrics and Elmer Press Inc. Journal website: https://theijcp.org/index.php/ijcp

8. Blaska, Joan K. (1998). Cyclical Grieving: Reoccurring Emotions Experienced by Parents Who Have Children with

Disabilities. Available at:
https://files.eric.ed.gov/fulltext/ED419349.pdf

9. Berger. D.S. Kids, Music 'n' Autism: Bringing out the Music in Your Child (2017) Jessica Kingsley Publishers, 73 Collier Street, London N1 9BE, UK and 400 Market Street, Suite 400, Philadelphia, PA 19106, USA. ISBN 978 1 78592 716 4, ISBN 978 1 78450 314 7

10. Brazier, Y. (2016). Autism: Parents face challenges, too. MEDICAL NEWS TODAY (2 November). Available at: https://www.medicalnewstoday.com/articles/313789.

11. Choosing between mainstream and a special school. (Last reviewed: 15 March 2016.) Available at: https://www.autism.org.uk/about/in-education/choosing-school/mainstream-special.aspx

12. Clark, T. Exploring Giftedness and Autism: A study of a differentiated educational program for autistic savants (2016. Routledge, 2 Park Square, Milton Park, Abingdon, Oxon, OX14 4LN, 711 Third Avenue, New York, NY 10017. ISBN: 978-1-138-83953-3, ISBN: 978-1-138-83954-0, ISBN: 978-1-315-73338-8.

13. Cook, E., Smith, V. and Brenner. M (2020) Parents' Experiences of Accessing Respite Care for Children with Autism Spectrum Disorder (ASD) at the Acute and Primary Care Interface a Systematic Review. Available at: https://www.ncbi.nlm.nih.gov/pmc/articles/PMC7243332/

14. Deweerdt, S. Culture: Diverse Diagnostics (2012). Available at: https://www.spectrumnews.org/news/culture-diverse-diagnostics/ [Accessed on 5th October 2020]

15. Dixon, R. The Management Task (2003) Butterworth=Heinemann. An imprint of Elsevier. Linacre House, Jordan Hill, Oxford OX2 8DP. 200 Wheeler Road, Burlington. MA 01808.

16. Dunbar, P. Penguin (2007) Walker Books. ISBN-13: 978-1-1406312461

17. Dunn, H, Mottram, H. Coombes, .E, Maclean, E. & Nugent, J foreword by Ockelford, A, Music Therapy and Autism Across the Lifespan: A Spectrum of Approaches (2019) Jessica Kingsley Publishers, 73 Collier Street, London N1 9BE, UK and 400 Market Street, Suite 400, Philadelphia, PA 19106, USA. ISBN 978 1 78592 311 1, ISBN 978 1 78450 622 3

18. En.wikipedia.org. 2020. Invictus [Online] Available at: https://en.wikipedia.org/wiki/Invictus [Accessed 24 September 2020]

19. Expert Advice and Support for Children with Speech and Language difficulties in Luton and Bedfordshire. Available at: https://childspeechbedfordshire.nhs.uk/specialism/tongue-tie/ [Accessed on 25th September 2020]

20. Elizabeth Kubler-Ross M.D On Death and Dying, Reprint Edition, (1997) Simon and Schuster, 1230 Ave of the America, New York, NY 10020, ISBN: 13978-0-684-83938-7

21. Fiske, K.E. Autism and the Family: Understanding and Supporting Parents and Siblings (2017) W.W. Norton & Company, Inc. 500 Fifth Avenue, New York, NY 10110. ISBN 978-0-393-71055-7.

22. Grant, R.J. Autoplay Therapy for Children and Adolescents on The Autism Spectrum – A Behaviour Plau-Based Approach, 3rd Edition. Routledge, 2 Park Square, Milton Park, Abingdon, Oxon, OX14 4LN, 711 Third Avenue, New York, NY 10017. ISBN: 978-1-138-10039-8, ISBN: 978-1-138-10040-4, ISBN: 978-1-315-65768-4

23. Grimes, D.R. Autism: how unorthodox treatments can exploit the vulnerable. The Guardian (Wed 15 Jul 2015 14.10 BST) available at https://www.theguardian.com/science/blog/2015/jul/15/autism-how-unorthodox-treatments-can-exploit-the-vulnerable

24. Halligan, E. My Child's Different: The lessons learned from one family's struggle to unlock their son's potential (2018). Crown House Publishing, Crown Building, Bancyfelin, Carmarthen, Wales, SA33 5ND, UK. www.crownhouse.co.uk and Crown House Publishing Company, LLC. PO.Box 2223, Willison, VT 05495, USA. www.crownhousepublishing.com. ISBN 978-178583328-1, ISBN 978-178583343-4, ISBN 978-178583344-1 and ISBN 978-178583345-8

25. Hannah, L. Teaching Young Children with Autistic Spectrum Disorders to Learn: A practical guide for parents and staff in general classrooms and preschool.

26. Hetzel, A. Ph.D Cyclical Grieving for Parents of Children with Autism (June 20, 2018) Available at https://www.hopebridge.com/blog/dr-anns-corner-cyclical-grieving-for-parents-of-children-with-autism/

27. Higham, P (2020) 2 Park Square, Milton Park, Abingdon, Oxon. OX14 4RN. ISBN 973-1—138-34294-1

28. Hirsch, L, MD (2016), Disciplining Your Child with Special Needs, kids' health, (September). Available at: https://kidshealth.org/en/parents/discipline-special.html

29. How to Help Your Non-verbal Child with Autism Speak (2017) https://otsimo.com/en/help-non-verbal-child-speak/

30. Hyman, S. & McIIwain (2019) Keeping Kids with Autism Safe from Wandering: Tips from the APP. Available at: https://www.healthychildren.org/English/health-issues/conditions/Autism/Pages/Autism-Wandering-Tips-AAP.aspx [Accessed on 05 October 2020]

31. I am autistic card Available at https://www.autism.org.uk/products/resources/alert-cards.aspx [Accessed on 27th July 2020]

32. Janis-Norton, N. Calmer, Easier, Happier Parenting: The Revolutionary Programme That Transforms Family Life (2016). Hodder & Stoughton Ltd, 338 Euston Road, London NW1 3BH. ISBN 978 1 444 7 29900, ISBN 978 1 444 7 29917

33. Kubler-Ross, E M.D On Death and Dying, Reprint Edition, (1997) Simon and Schuster, 1230 Ave of the America, New York, NY 10020, ISBN: 13978-0-684-83938-7

34. Promoting an awareness of autism. Available at https://www.thedtgroup.org/autism-and-learning-disabilities/promoting-an-awareness-of-autism [Accessed on 1st October 2020]

35. Maurice. C. Let Me Hear Your Voice: A Family's Triumph Over Autism: Written by Catherine Maurice (1998) Robert Hale Limited. Clerkenwell House, Clerkenwell Green, London. EC1R 0HT.

36. Mbele, J. Africans and Americans: Embracing Cultural Differences (2011). https://www.lulu.com/content/105001 ISBN – 13: 978-1411623415

37. Meadan, H., Halle, J. W., & Ebata, A. T. (2010). Families with children who have autism spectrum disorders: Stress and support. Exceptional Children, 77(1), 7-36. Retrieved from the ERIC database.

38. Melinda Smith, M.A., Jeanne Segal, Ph.D., and Ted Hutman, PhD. Last updated: November 2019. Helping Your Child with Autism Thrive Available at

https://www.helpguide.org/articles/autism-learning-disabilities/helping-your-child-with-autism-thrive.htm

39. Nakra, O (2018) Understanding Autism: A Guide for Parents and Teachers, Norton Press, Chennai. ISBN 978=1-64428-596-0

40. Nasen, B. The Autism Discussion Page on the core challenges of autism: A toolbox for helping children with autism feel safe, accepted, and competent. (2014). Jessica Kingsley Publishers. ISBN-13: 978-1849059947

41. Newton, J. Amazing Grace. Available at https://en.wikipedia.org/wiki/Amazing_Grace [Accessed on 25th September 2020]

42. Notbohm, E. Ten Things Every Child with Autism Wishes You Knew, 3rd Edition (2019) Future Horizon, 721 W. Abram Street, Arlington, TX.76013. ISBN 9781941765883.

43. Ockelford, A. Music, Language and Autism: Exceptional Strategies for Exceptional Minds (2013) Jessica Kingsley Publishers, 116 Pentonville Road, London N1 9JB, UK and 400 Market Street, Suite, 400 Philadelphia, PA 19106, USA. ISBN 978 1 84905 187 2 ISBN 978 1 95700 428 4.

44. Position statement: therapies and interventions – National Autistic Society. Available at: https://www.autism.org.uk/get-involved/media-centre/position-statements/interventions.aspx

45. Rogers, W.S. Social Psychology. (2011) 2nd Ed. Open University Press. ISBN-13: 978-0-33-5240999-9

46. Rudy L.J. medically reviewed by Snyder C. MD Coping with Grief After an Autism Diagnosis November 05, 2019, Available at https://www.verywellhealth.com/coping-with-grief-after-an-autism-diagnosis-260273

47. Ryan, S. 'Meltdowns', surveillance and managing emotions; going out with children with autism Science Direct Volume 16, Issue 5, September 2010, Pages 868-875 available at https://www.sciencedirect.com/science/article/pii/S1353829 210000572

48. Sensory Differences. Avaialable at: https://www.autismtas.org.au/about-autism/key-areas-of-difference/sensory-differences/#:~:text=Many%20people%20with%20autism%20have,one%20day%20to%20the%20next [Accessed on 30th September 2020]

49. Shea, L., Frankish, M. and Frabkish. S (2019) Understanding and Managing Pica. Available at: https://network.autism.org.uk/knowledge/insight-opinion/understanding-and-managing-pica [Accessed on 25th September 2020]

50. Speech and Feeding Improvements in Children After Posterior Tongue-Tie Release: A Case Series Volume 7, Number 3, September 2018, pages 29-35 Available at https://www.theijcp.org/index.php/ijcp/article/view/295/254

51. Signs and Symptoms of Autism Spectrum Disorders (2019) Available at https://www.cdc.gov/ncbddd/autism/signs.html

52. The Cause of Autism, (2020). Available at: https://www.autism.org.uk/advice-and-guidance/what-is-autism/the-causes-of-autism

53. Tongue Tie - Advice for parents and carers of babies born with a tongue tie (Ankyloglossia) Speech and Language Therapy Service. 1 April 2018 Available at https://www.cambscommunityservices.nhs.uk/docs/default-source/Beds---SLT/0528---tongue-tie.pdf?sfvrsn=2

54. Warrell, M. You've Got This! The Life-changing Power of Trusting Yourself (2020) John Wiley & Sons Australia Ltd.

42 McDougall St. Milton Qld 4064. ISBN: 978-0-730-36844-1

55. What is Autism. Available at :
https://www.autism.org.uk/advice-and-guidance/what-is-autism

56. Transition to the new 0 to 25 special educational needs and disability system. Departmental advice for local authorities and their partner. 3rd Edition (2014). Available at: https://www.bl.uk/collection-items/transition-to-the-new-0-to-25-special-educational-needs-and-disability-system-departmental-advice-for-local-authorities-and-their-partners-third-edition [Accessed 02 October 2020)

57. What is the Local Offer, Available at https://www.leicestershire.gov.uk/education-and-children/special-educational-needs-and-disability/where-to-start-with-send/what-is-the-local-offer

58. Wandering. Available at https://nationalautismassociation.org/resources/awaare-wandering/#:~:text=ASD%20wandering%20behaviors%20happen%20under,or%20away%20from%20something%20bothersome. [Accessed on 02 October 2020]

ACKNOWLEDGEMENT

Many waters cannot quench love; rivers cannot sweep it away. if one were to give all the wealth of one's house for love. It would be utterly scorned.
Song of Solomon 8:7

To my father Chief T.A Esan. I appreciate you for who you are and for all the great lessons you took time to stamp upon my heart and most importantly, for letting me know that if I dare to fly, the sky is not even the limit.

I want to thank my husband, Idowu Adekunle Adesokan who has been my co-pilot in this journey as each day unfolds. Together we have experienced the highs and lows, but never did I see you give up. Thank you for all you do for me and the children. To my daughter Ademurewa, I look forward to seeing all the stories you write travelling the world.

I want to appreciate my siblings by blood and by law who have held my hands when I thought I could no longer go on. You gave me hope, you believe in me and you are always there for me in ways beyond my comprehension. I could not have asked for better siblings than you. I want you to know, I greatly appreciate every one of you. Thank you for standing rock-solid for me.

For my friends and family who read through the draft of the different stages, cumulating in the publication of this book, your constructive advice and insightful input means a lot to me. Thank you for investing your time and thoughts into making this book a reality. Even if I do not mention you by name, you know yourselves and I appreciate every one of you.

I want to thank EVERYONE who ever said anything positive about my writing and EVERYONE who encouraged me to keep on writing hoping that one day, I will write a book. I want you to know I took it all to heart and this book bears testimony to your kind words.

Much appreciation goes to Adegbemiro. Being a mother to you has taught me the true meaning of grit, faith, empathy, motivation, and resilience. You never cease to amaze me as you continue to grow in leap and bounds. You have smashed so many limits that we thought will hold you down like gravity. So, my son, always remembers the words of Kevin Keenon that say, "When they say you can't, they show you their limits, not yours." For you, Ade is destined for great heights.

To the many families living with autism who often live in a secret world, where parents/caregivers may have to put on a bold face playing the superheroes to their children with autism. Today, I acknowledge you for pouring out your heart, mind, soul, and body for your precious jewels. Thank you for striving daily to ensure that your children have the best life outcomes possible despite autism. I salute you and I hear you. So, keep your record on.

Above all, I want to thank you God Almighty. My rock, my shield, my strength, my song, and the lover of my soul. Without You, there is simply no me!

NOTE FROM THE AUTHOR.

I hope you have found this book beneficial in one way or the other. If so, then please leave a review. Your review will make the text more visible and accessible to others who may also benefit from it.

You can connect with me on Twitter @AdesokanToyin, on Instagram @ toyinesanadesokan, and Facebook @ Adesola Toyin Esan Adesokan

Thank you,

Adesola Toyin Adesokan